# Having It All

## Body, Mind, Heart & Spirit Together Again at Last

**Phil Porter**

**with Cynthia Winton–Henry**

*Published by*

**WING IT! Press**

**669A 24th Street**

**Oakland, CA 94612**

phone   510/465–2797

fax   510/836–3312

email   pporter316@aol.com

ISBN   0–9636755–1–6

Library of Congress Catalog Card Number: 97–90211

Book Design:  Phil Porter

Photos, pp. 4, 50, 104: Steve Savage (415/626–2610)

Other photos: Mike Walker, Phil Porter, Cynthia Winton–Henry

Thank you to InterPlayers who appear in photos: Pat Littman, Fawn Christianson, Susanne Mulcahy, Ted Thompson, Krista Gemmel Harris, Chuck Graham, Leah Mann, Beth Hoch, David McCauley, Penny Mann, Frieder Mann, Amber Walker, Betsy Lurie, Masankho Banda, Annegret Zander, Laurie Rudel, Lynn Webber, and Stephen Winton–Henry

# Having It All

## Body, Mind, Heart & Spirit Together Again At Last

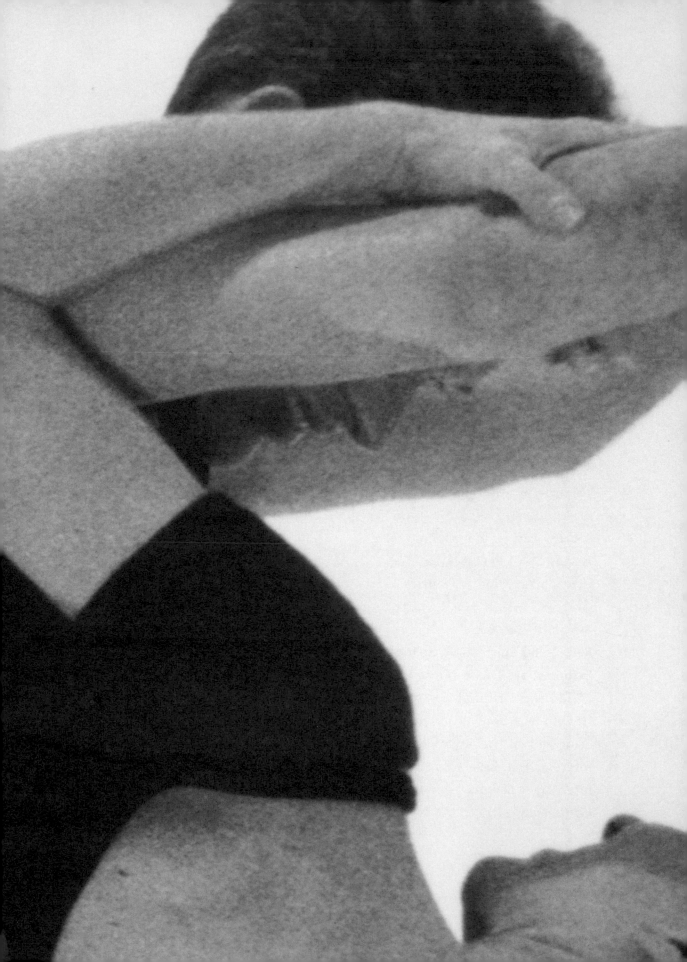

# Introduction

**What do you want?**

More energy?

More grace?

More joy?

More community?

More fun?

More peace?

More connection?

More spirit?

**You can have more.** Your life can be full.

**This book will tell you how.**

Here you will find ways to change your life. Some may be easy, others more challenging. Most will require practice, but some changes will be effortless to make. You can choose what is helpful for you and discard the rest.

This book includes new ways of looking at or thinking about your life, but you don't need to throw out what you already know. You don't have to change overnight, you don't need a new wardrobe or heavy equipment to follow this advice. **It is up to you**.

**The ideas found in this book are rooted in a practice called InterPlay that my colleague Cynthia Winton–Henry and I have developed over the last 15 years.** InterPlay takes the best from art, church, and therapy. It playfully reintegrates body and spirit through new ideas and practices and is dedicated to community building, artfulness, fun, and transformation for anyone. (You will find more of our story and more about the practice of InterPlay in three chapters near the end of this book: "Dancing into the Age of Reintegration," "InterPlay is a Great Way to Have It All," and "InterPlay & Lessons about Life.")

We have been teaching and leading groups all over the country and in other parts of the world, and our experience with people of all shapes and sizes has shaped and refined our philosophy. **We believe that these ideas are powerful because they are rooted in experience and practice.** Ideas alone are not enough. What will we do with them? How will we use them to change our lives?

There is plenty of advice to help you change your life offered here. **It is important for you to remember that you have choices about the information that you read: you can choose which advice to heed.** You may not agree with our view of the "way things are" or "the way things ought to be." You may find that some tools are more helpful than others, or that one principle makes more sense than another. You may need to find or invent your own specific practices.

**We also encourage an attitude of ease and amusement in life, to the process of change, and even to the information in this book.** The advice may seem strong, but you are free to hold it lightly.

**Part of "having it all" is reclaiming your inner authority—the part of you that knows who you are, what you like, what you want, and what you know.** One way to begin reclaiming your inner authority is to carefully compare our information with your own experience and question our conclusions if they don't match up. When you do this, you honor your own life and experience. **In short, you're on your way to having it all!**

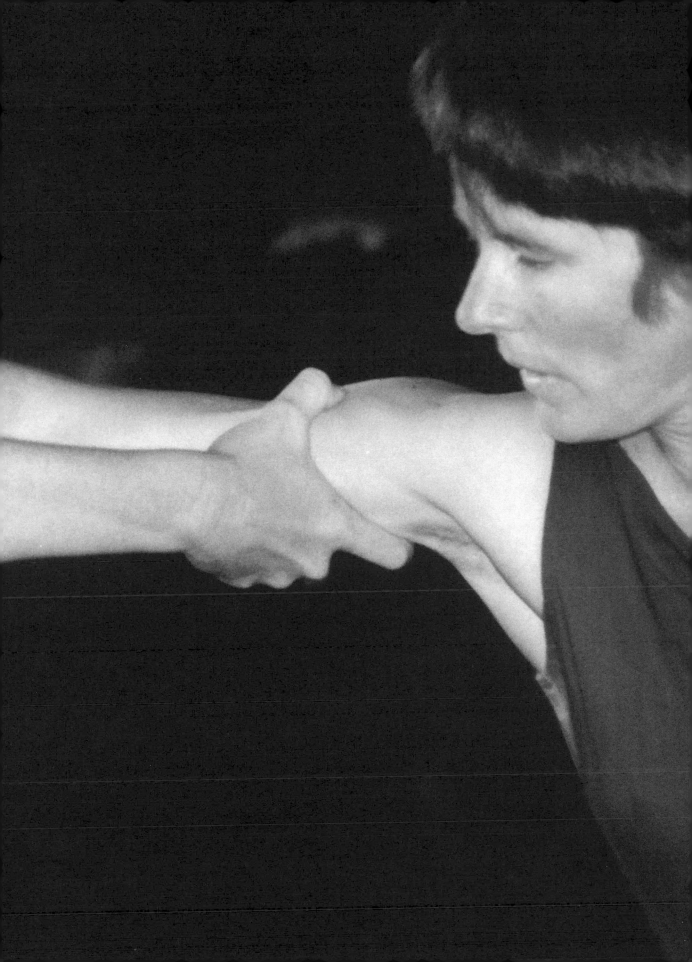

# The Body/Mind/Heart/Spirit Split

**A D V I C E**   *Notice how often you and others use these four categories—mind, body, heart, spirit—to describe human experience.*

**In our culture, we take our experience and divide it into four neat boxes: body, mind, heart, spirit. Then we store the boxes on separate shelves far away from each other, perhaps even in warehouses in cities miles apart. We are utterly convinced that our lives are that neat and tidy and the distinctions are that clear.**

Despite all the writing, preaching, and teaching going on in our culture right now about integrating the different parts of ourselves, no one questions these categories which we have used for so long to understand our experience. What if this system of categories is itself keeping us from having wholeness? What if it doesn't really match our experience?

**The body/mind/heart/spirit system is a construct, a particular way of thinking and talking about experience.** But it does more than describe. It shapes experience as well. If we take for granted not only the existence of these categories but also their simplicity and neatness, then we will continue to try to shove our experience into these boxes, even if it wants to merge, flow, or spill over. Can we have "spirit" at work, "body" at church, "heart" in the science lab?

Let me suggest an analogy:

In almost every kitchen you will find a drawer that has silverware in it, usually with one of those dividers that keeps the knives, forks, and spoons separate. Silverware is easy to organize, easy to tell apart. You may even have your silverware neatly stacked, with each piece pointing in the same direction. We treat our experience like the silverware drawer. **We focus on the knives, forks, and spoons of our experience, and we believe that it is all as easy as that to sort and organize.**

> • • • • • • • • •
> **Our lives are actually more like the sum total of all of the items in all the drawers in the kitchen....Some of our experience is as simple as a knife or fork, but mostly it is not.**

But don't you also have a drawer in your kitchen that has all the weird utensils and odd items that you know will come in handy one day: the garlic press, the potato masher, the chopsticks you brought home from the Chinese restaurant, the fuses, and the garbage bag ties? How do we sort these odds and ends?

Our lives are actually more like the sum total of all of the items in all the drawers in the kitchen (and while we are at it we better throw in everything we have stored in the office, bedroom, basement, and garage as well.) Some of our experience is as simple as a knife or fork, but mostly it is not. And in order to have full lives, we need more than those simple elements. We need the paring knives and wire whisks and cheese graters of our experience as well. **We need all of our experience whether we can categorize it or not.**

The body/mind/heart/spirit construct may be part of the problem. It may be keeping us from wholeness. This book is about looking at our experience in new ways. **Even more, though, it is about *having* our experience—having it all.**

We will pay extra attention to the split between body and spirit in this book, because these two categories seem to be so difficult to integrate. To understand how we can transcend the boundaries between these two categories will show us how we can integrate any or all of them.

You may have noticed that you focus or emphasize one of these categories over others. You may pay more attention to feeling than thinking, or you may focus a great deal on spirit. It is important to affirm this strength, even as you learn that you can have all of your experience fully.

 **R E S U L T S** *To acknowledge how the body/mind/heart/ spirit construct shapes our experience will be the first step toward having a more unified, integrated view of our experience.*

• • • • • • • • • • • • • • • • • • • • • • •

*It isn't easy to be all of me all of the time. In any particular situation there is something about who I am that the people I am with would find hard to believe. Do you ever have that experience?*

*Wherever I am, there is some little piece of myself that I quietly keep under wraps: the person who dances, the person who prays, the person who picks his nose or has uncharitable thoughts, the person who makes love, or the one who spends hours in front of the computer. Perhaps that is why I choose to live in a big city, where there are different locations to be different parts of myself.*

*On the other hand, I know I need to be known in all my incongruous entirety. And I am. There are more and more people in my life who know the many sides of me, and I am happier for that.*

*I know deep inside that all the parts fit together into one whole. The conflict I or others see between the parts is externally imposed. I need all of me wherever I am, even if I can't fully acknowledge that with the ones I am with.*

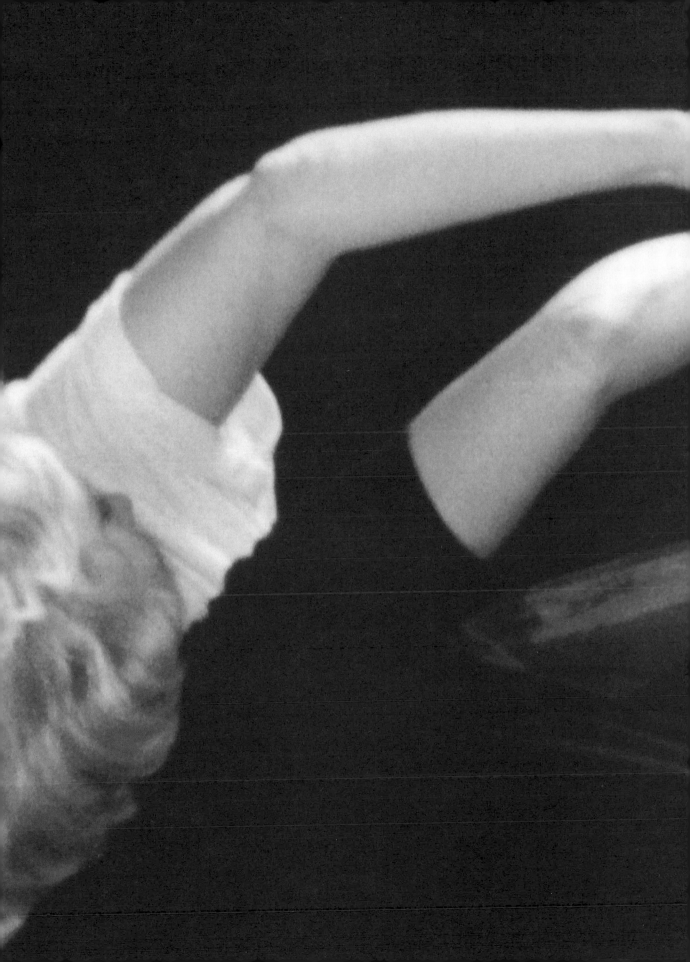

# Our Experience Is Complex

**ADVICE**  *The first step toward "having it all" is to realize just how broad the range of our experience is.*

Our physical experience is complex and textured. The following is a list of over a hundred common words describing certain experiences. Can you identify these in yourself or others? Are they familiar experiences to you?

| | | |
|---|---|---|
| abundance | aggression | aimlessness |
| anger | anticipation | anxiety |
| arousal | articulation | attraction |
| awe | balance | beauty |
| bitchiness | charisma | charm |
| clarity | clumsiness | community |
| companionship | competence | conceit |
| concern | confusion | conservatism |
| containment | delight | déjà vu |
| depression | desire | deviousness |
| dignity | disjointedness | dread |
| elegance | embarrassment | envy |
| excellence | expansiveness | expectation |
| exhilaration | fear | home |
| elation | energy | enlightenment |
| entrancement | fanaticism | forethought |
| fullness | generosity | grace |
| guilt | handsomeness | health |
| hope | hospitality | humility |
| imagination | insight | intelligence |
| intuition | jerkiness | jumpiness |
| kindness | love | manic |
| memory | mastery | meanness |

| | | |
|---|---|---|
| nausea | nervousness | obstinacy |
| organization | orderliness | peace |
| perfectionism | possessiveness | prayerfulness |
| presence | pride | purposefulness |
| rambling | relaxation | repentance |
| repression | reverence | roughness |
| sacrifice | sadness | servility |
| sexiness | sluggishness | shyness |
| sincerity | smoothness | stiffness |
| stress | stubbornness | survival |
| threat | trust | understanding |
| vanity | wonder | |

There are many of them, aren't there? Some of these may also have variations or different levels of intensity. Some have been left out entirely. Can you imagine how long the list could get? What words would you add to the list?

Now try these experiments:

1. Go through the list and assign each of these experiences to one of the four categories—"mind," "body," "heart," or "spirit."

2. Pick a few of these words and imagine how they might fit in any or all of the other categories.

3. Look at each of the words on the list and think about the physical experience of each one.

What did you notice in this process?

You may have noticed how difficult it is to describe how some of these experiences feel in our bodies.

You may have noticed that some of the words were easy to stick in a category but others wanted to perch between two or more categories.

You may have noticed that you could make a case for assigning some of these to different categories than you first chose.

Hopefully you noticed elements of physicality in many, if not all, of these words.

What else did you notice? Make a list of your observations, even if they aren't directly related to the purpose of the exercise, or if they seem completely personal.

If you try this experiment with a friend, you may notice that you don't always agree on where a word should be placed—different people have different experiences.

**To notice your own information—thoughts, feelings, sensations, ideas, energy, reactions—is an important step in the process of claiming your inner authority**. Interesting or surprising information may pop up at unexpected moments. It is important to grab it right when it happens regardless of the context. Learn what there is for you to learn.

**RESULTS**   *To realize how full the range of our experience is and how easily our experience slides between and among the categories of spirit, heart, body, and mind will help us have the marvelous interconnectedness of the bits and pieces of our lives.*

• • • • • • • • • • • • • • • • • • • •

*I was taking a theater improvisation class many years ago. There was an exercise we did in which two people created a scene together while two other people called out names of emotions that they were to portray within this interaction. Every time a new feeling was called out the improviser had to quickly shift his or her portrayal. In the beginning, the emotions were fairly standard—happy, sad, confused, angry, frustrated—but as the exercise went on that night they got more and more creative. Even though this was years ago, I clearly remember someone calling out the word "mystical." I could tell that the whole group noticed the strange-*

*ness of including this word as an "emotion"—a palpable "huh?" registered in the group. It obviously had meaning of one sort or another, but it wasn't exactly what we would normally call a "feeling." And how would it be acted out?*

*I think this was one of the first clues that I got about how fuzzy categories can be and how complex our experience is. As we started naming emotions, we named the easy ones—the ones that fit neatly in the box. But it wasn't long before we were getting near the edge, in territory that is much more difficult to define.*

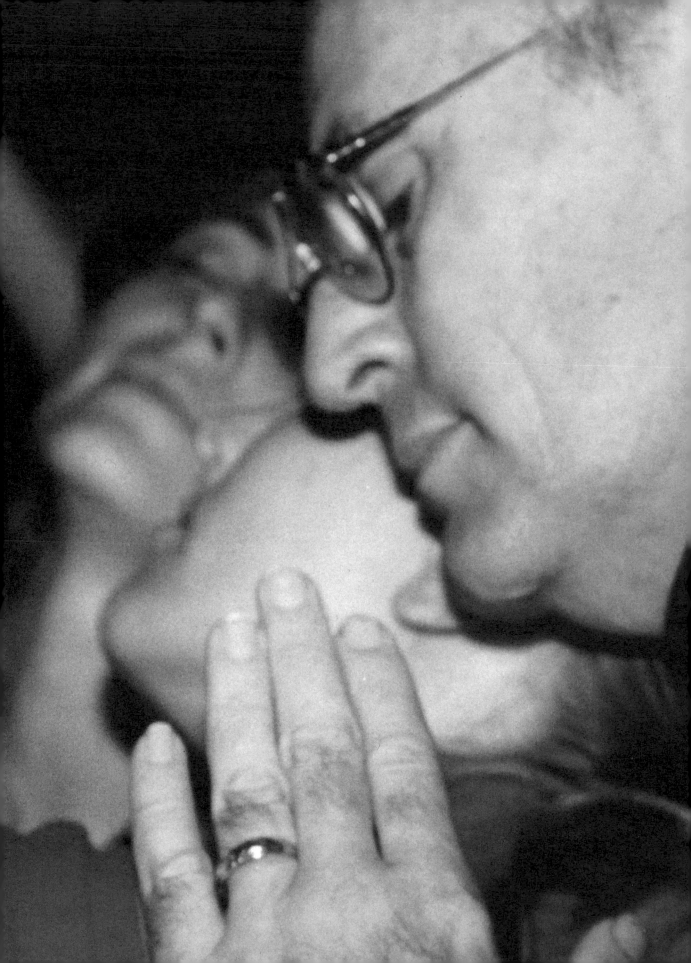

# Physicality Is Basic

**ADVICE** *Change your view of physicality and you will experience more integration.*

The first step toward the process of integration—to breaking down the barriers between body, spirit, mind, and heart—is to claim the physicality of all experience. **Physicality is basic.**

We do not *have* bodies, we *are* bodies. All of our experience is physical. Feelings are physical, spirituality is physical, thinking is physical. All of the stuff going on in and around us is physical. How would we know that anything was going on if there weren't some sort of experience that was noticeable to us?

**Our experience is complex, multilayered, and completely intertwined.** We fool ourselves if we think we can neatly organize it. Our experience is like a tapestry. We can pick it apart and examine separate threads, but it makes the most sense and is the most beautiful when we see it as a whole.

Have you noticed any of these things?

- that we identify "feelings" by their physical sensations or our behavior? (body/heart)

- that when your body is sluggish it is harder to pay attention? (body/mind)

- that when you come across an exciting idea your body gets energized?(body/mind)

- that sometimes scientific explanations just don't seem sufficient? (mind/heart)

- that crying in a movie feels good? (body/heart)

- that "anticipation" can include elements of dread or elements of excitement, or both? (heart/body)

- that you can "think" and "feel" at the same time? (heart/mind)

- that trust has to do with your willingness to "fall"? (heart/body)

- that sometimes answers come when you are not focusing on the questions? (mind/spirit)

- that "spiritual" experience can happen in unexpected places—at work, on the beach, or while having sex? (spirit/body)

- that people disagree about exactly how hot the chili should be? (body/mind)

- that when you arrange the furniture in the room one way it is more satisfying than another? (body/heart)

- that some people like classical music and some people like jazz? (body/heart/mind/spirit)

- that it is difficult to put into words what a Mozart composition "means" but that it makes sense anyway? (mind/heart/body/spirit)

- that you can know when something is just right, even if you can't explain why? (heart/mind)

- that everyone's handwriting is different? (body/spirit)

- that two people can describe the same event in completely different ways? (mind/heart/body)

- that you can know a lot about someone just from looking at them? (body/spirit)

- that you can recognize when you are "in love"? (body/mind/heart/spirit)

- that the way food looks affects its appeal? (mind/body)

- that exercise can clear your "mind" and that sometimes you have more energy after exercising than before you started? (body/mind)

I have indicated how these experiences overlap categories.

These could be debated. But this list helps us see how intertwined our experience is. Perhaps it will help us release our grip on this limiting body/heart/mind/spirit construct.

**RESULTS** *When you claim the wholeness of your experience—the ways in which everything is interrelated and intertwined—you reclaim the rich texture of your life.*

• • • • • • • • • • • • • • • • • • • • • • •

*I'm not convinced that "thinking" really happens inside my skull. Except for headaches, I really don't have much physical sensation in that portion of my body.*

*I think we think of thinking as happening up there because our eyes and ears are so close by. Much of what we call thinking involves visual or auditory memory or imagination. Since these major sense organs are right up there at the top of our heads, we ascribe thinking to that location.*

*Remember the section on human anatomy in the encyclopedia? It had several layers printed on some wonderful see–through material. As you turned them one at a time you could see the different systems in the body. Remember the page with the nervous system on it? It wasn't just an isolated brain, but a whole network of red, snaky nerves that traveled to every portion of the body, right down to the fingertips and toes. You have brains in your whole body: brains in your hands, your thighs, your elbows, your nostrils.*

*Try this experiment: make a shape with one hand. Change it to another shape. Now change it five times really quickly. Your hand can change faster than you "think."*

*What would happen if we used the brains in our whole body?*

# Claim It
# Even If You Can't
# Articulate It

**ADVICE** *If you can't explain your experience, don't worry about it. You can "have" it anyway.*

Often we lack the words to describe our experience. Can we really describe our feelings about our children? Can we say why we trust someone from the moment that we meet them? Can we explain what it is like to be one with all of creation? Can we truly describe dizziness?

This is the first corollary to the principle that physicality is basic: **you don't have to be able to articulate your experience in order to claim it.** You do not need to be able to put it into words in order for it to be real.

> • • • • • • • • •
>
> **You can be in love even if you can't describe the feeling. You can trust your instincts or intuition. You can like one color more than another even if you don't know why. You can have God even if you can't explain God.**

You can be in love even if you can't describe the feeling. You can trust your instincts or intuition. You can like one color more than another even if you don't know why. You can have God even if you can't explain God.

Our culture has a hard time with this. We want explanations, quantification, and proof, especially if something is even slightly out of the ordinary. That is why it is so important for each of us to claim the authority of our experience. We need this inner strength and wisdom in the face of a suspicious culture.

........
**21**

**RESULTS** *Everyone has experience they can't describe. It can be wondrous, awe–inspiring, deeply moving, scary, subtle, or minute, **and** impossible to wrap up in words. We can still acknowledge and enjoy, or just **experience** these moments— "have" them. Our lives will be richer for it.*

• • • • • • • • • • • • • • • • • • • • • • •

*I was watching the broadcast of the Tony Awards, the ones given to Broadway shows, on television one evening a few years ago. Each year they stage scenes from several of the nominated plays or musicals. This particular year Stephen Sondheim's musical* Sunday in the Park with George *was nominated. It is the story of Georges Seurat, the French "pointillist" painter. He built up his paintings with tiny little dots of color.*

*The scene presented from the musical begins with a bare stage. As the music plays, the elements of this one painting, for which Seurat is most famous, begin to appear three–dimensionally. It is the painting of people posed rather formally in a park near the water. Some of the elements in the staged version are painted backdrops that move into place from all directions, others are live bodies, but gradually the entire scene is recreated.*

*The music is slowly building along with the image of the paint-ing. As the image is completed, the music ends with a series of the most haunting, transcendent chords that I have ever heard. The music was new to me and I was transfixed. Just thinking about these final sounds—replaying them in my imagination— makes shivers run up and down my spine.*

*What is it about certain images or sounds or sights that can move us so? There are many passages of music that I have come to cherish as I have listened to them over and over, but this piece hit me from the first time I heard it. Other music seems to affect me viscerally, but this had a quality of spirit to it that I can't real-ly explain. What language speaks to us in these sounds? And to what part of our bodyspirit does it speak?*

*We all have these experiences from time to time, don't we? I hope we can grab them when they come. Perhaps it is their in-utterability that makes them so powerful.*

........
**23**

# Body Data, Knowledge & Wisdom

 **ADVICE** *Become more aware of your inner information—what you notice in the moment, the patterns in your experience, and the choices you make based on this information.*

**Our lives are full of physical information and experience, much of which we ignore.** We can learn to pay closer attention to our inner information. Here are three steps you can use in the process:

1. Notice the **information** that is occurring in the moment: **body data**.

2. Notice the **patterns** in your information over time: **body knowledge**.

3. Use your body knowledge to **structure** your life and make **choices** in a way that is beneficial to yourself and/or others, the earth, or all of creation (God): **body wisdom**.

**"Body data" are immediate, present–time bits of information:** I am cold, I am hungry, my back hurts, I am worried about tomorrow's meeting, I remember sitting in the auditorium the day I graduated, I am excited about seeing a friend, I hear the rain outside.

**This information comes to us constantly, one piece overlapping another.** We ignore most of it, paying attention to only a little at a time. For example, right now there are sensations coming from the back of your left knee, but you probably wouldn't have noticed it if I hadn't pointed it out. **Even though we can only focus on one piece at time, many things are happening in each moment, including present time connections to the past and future.** What body data do you notice right now? Are you hot, cold, energized, relaxed, any pains or discomfort, worries, anticipation, memories? This is all body data.

**If you pay attention, you will see patterns in your body data. This is what we call "body knowledge."**
Here are some examples: you prefer jazz music to classical, purple is your favorite color, you are more alert in the morning than in the evening, you are sexually attracted to redheads, you are good at organizing large groups of people, you are afraid of heights, you prefer taking a shower to taking a bath.

> ● ● ● ● ● ● ● ● ●
> **If you know you are good at organizing large groups of people but hate dealing with money, then you should be a chairperson and not a treasurer. If you hate making phone calls, you should avoid telephone sales positions.**

What are your habits or preferences in any area of your life? What brings you pleasure? What drives you crazy? Who do you like to be with? What parts of your job do you like the best? What gives you energy? What do you choose to do when you have a choice? This is all body knowledge—seeing the patterns in body data.

**"Body wisdom" is the use of our body knowledge to structure our lives in ways that are beneficial: to us, to others, to the earth, or to all of creation (God).**
Body wisdom can be simple, profound, or both. If, for example, you know you are a "morning person," you should organize things so that you are doing the most demanding or creative work at that time of the day. If you know you are good at organizing large groups of people but hate dealing with money, then you should be a chair-

person and not a treasurer. If you hate making phone calls, you should avoid telephone sales positions. If you need time alone to have a sense of balance, you should create that for yourself. If you know that a trip to the gym will be good for your health, you should get there, even if it seems like hard work. If you know that driving your car pollutes the air, you should drive it less.

Don't waste your body knowledge—use it. It is good to know what our patterns are, but it is great when we can use this information to create better lives.

Can we make choices for our own good? We have been taught that self–indulgence is bad. We shouldn't do things for our own pleasure or satisfaction. We should only think about others' needs. This is a split. **Actually, we can shape our lives in ways that are good for ourselves and others.** And we can extend our range of concern as far as we choose. How far does your circle of concern go? Who does it include? Family and friends? Your community? People in other parts of the world? Can it include the good of the earth? Can it include infinity, the cosmos, God? This is your choice.

**It is important to remember that body wisdom is rooted in the details of our experience, the bits and pieces of everyday life.** You can't gain body wisdom without gathering the data and noticing the patterns. We may learn from others, but the most powerful body wisdom comes from our own experience.

**R E S U L T S** *Paying attention to your own information increases inner authority, which is a crucial balance to external information and control. By paying attention you will be more able to make choices that will be good for you and others.*

●●●●●●●●●●●●●●●●●●●●●●●

*I hate waiting. I even hate waiting to fall asleep. I read until I doze off. I know that as soon as I put the book down and turn off the light I will fall asleep immediately. I like to sleep in a particular position with the pillows just the right way. I sleep best when I am cool but not cold.*

*I know that although I am capable of getting up when an alarm rings, I much prefer getting up simply when I awake. Since I am self–employed, I go to bed when I am tired and get up when I am ready. I am on a quite regular sleeping schedule, and I get up at a reasonable hour each day. But for all intents and purposes, I get to sleep in every day.*

*I discovered in recent conversations with several people that they each had very specific body knowledge about their personal sleeping habits. They also knew when they were most tired and when they were most alert. I asked them how many were in work situations where they were forced to be on a schedule that was in direct conflict with their "sleep" body knowledge. Most of the group raised their hands.*

*I think there is a strong thread in our culture that says we can't expect to sleep when we want to. Those who are parents know the meaning of sleep deprivation; work schedules take precedence over our personal sleep patterns. Should we expect otherwise?*

*But what would happen if we took our body knowledge about sleep to the level of body wisdom? What if we organized our working lives around the optimal patterns of our energy, including our need to sleep? Wouldn't we be both happier and more productive?*

# The Tyranny of External Information

**A D V I C E** *Learn the difference between what others have taught you and what you have learned from your own experience. This is one of the most important tasks in the process of understanding our own physicality.*

We all carry lots of information around with us in our bodies. Most of it is not our own—it has been poured into us by parents, teachers, religious leaders, and the media. Some of it has taken such strong hold in us that we don't even know that it isn't our own information. **We have been persuaded, influenced, inculturated, indoctrinated, even brainwashed.**

It is a normal part of growing up in any particular family, community, or culture to pick up the customs and patterns of those around us or have them drilled into us. We receive this external information in a variety of ways.

Some messages are clearly repeated to us over and over again: pick up your clothes, get your elbows off the table, look both ways before you cross the street, don't litter, buy this toilet paper, be all you can be. **Messages that we hear so frequently can hardly help but become part of our own information.** Advertisers in particular have exploited the way our bodies take in information.

Other "lessons" are more subtly communicated. We may learn them from observing others, or they may be implied. For example, we may pick up messages about the way that others react to us and then form pictures of ourselves that may or may not be accurate: "I'm too loud" or "I am not attractive enough." Our reactions to people of other racial or ethnic groups may be based on overt comments we have heard, but they may also be based on much less direct information that we pick up in our homes or communities. Until we began to see more women doctors, either real or portrayed on television, we may have believed that they were not qualified for the medical profession.

**There is also a difference between seeing a portrayal of a particular experience and having experience.** For example, I have never personally witnessed a murder, but I have seen hundreds of people killed on television and in the movies. I have never been to the former Soviet Union, but as I was growing up I was given information about the country and its people that was distorted. It is easy to confuse indirect experiences with direct ones. Portrayals are not the same as actual experience.

Why is it important to be able to distinguish between external and internal information, between body wisdom and indoctrination? There are several reasons:

- **What we have been taught may simply not match our own body needs.** I may have been trained to go to bed early when it really works best for me if I stay up late and then sleep in. I may have been discouraged from pursuing an interest or career that was important for me to follow. I may have been taught to do things a certain way when there are better ways for me to do them.

- **Information that comes from the media is often distorted.** A murder on television is usually tastefully lighted and accompanied by dramatic music. This is different from real life. A single incident played up in the media often takes on dramatic proportions, even if it is an isolated event.

- **Some of what we have been taught to believe may not match current realities.** The times are changing quickly—can we? New realities may conflict with deeply ingrained information. And you may be part of a group that desires that kind of change: if you are a woman, you may want to be a completely different sort of person than you were brought up to be; if you are an environmentalist, you may want others to shift their fundamental understanding of the earth.

- **External information is often purposely manipulative.** Other people want us to behave in certain ways for their own benefit. To be able to compare external information with our own body wisdom can keep us from being used in ways we want to avoid.

**If you are unable to sort out the difference between body wisdom and indoctrination, you will lack an ability to make choices in certain areas of your life.** "It is more important to stay in my marriage than to escape abuse." "Women don't become physicists." "People won't like me if I have strong opinions." It is quite possible to honor what we have been taught, or what our communities believe, and have the power of our own body wisdom. For example, we may choose to participate in a family tradition of having a large Thanksgiving meal, even though we might personally prefer a simple meal with one other person.

To recognize these deeply embedded cultural messages does not necessarily mean rejecting them. To have the ability to recognize them adds to our sense of inner authority. It increases the likelihood that we will make choices that are good for ourselves and others. Life decisions based only on external information may be bad for us.

**There are relatively few settings where our own sense of authority—what we know to be true for ourselves—is being developed or affirmed.**

In particular we are not taught to trust the information of our own bodies: to notice the details of our physicality, to recognize the patterns, to shape our lives according to our inner wisdom. We are suspicious of any information that is difficult to articulate. We are not taught to differentiate between information that is our own and that which has been drilled into us.

**If we are to have lives that are "more"—full, abundant, and healthy—we must have a firm sense of our own inner authority.** We must practice noticing and honoring our own information. This is particularly important in a world where so much information is being poured into us from the outside.

Don't be surprised if it feels like a lonely task to claim your own information. Unfortunately, in our culture there aren't many situations or systems where our inner authority is validated. You may need to look specifically for individuals or groups of people who will support you, people who will listen to your experience and affirm it.

 **RESULTS** *If you know the difference between what others have taught you and what you know from your own experience, it will be easier to make good life choices, especially when the two conflict. To ignore your own information can be dangerous to your well-being.*

● ● ● ● ● ● ● ● ● ● ● ● ● ● ● ● ● ● ●

*The other day in the bookstore, I picked up a self–help book by one of the more prominent gurus and thumbed through it. I happened onto a section that talked about research that was done on rabbits showing that those who received more physical contact were healthier. The author used this research to suggest that the same would be true for humans—that we all could use more touch and affection.*

*I noticed that my blood began to simmer. Do we really need the scientific community to confirm the value of touch and affection? Are we so out of touch from our own experience to know that most of us need lots of physical reassurance? Does a scientist have to prove it for us first in the laboratory? With rabbits?*

*Do we need the scientific community to prove that prayer can be healing for some, that women should be able to give birth in a comforting environment surrounded by people she loves, that singing is good for us, or that including "spirit" in the workplace might be good for employees and employers alike?*

*I fully appreciate the knowledge that science has brought into the world. But what about wisdom? Wisdom is firmly based in experience. It doesn't require empirical confirmation. Can we claim what we know is true and right and good regardless of whether it can be proven? Can we recognize those within our communities who are wise and have wisdom to share?*

*Look around you. Who are the people in your life who are wise? Are you?*

# "Pictures" Can Cloud Our View

**A D V I C E**  *Understand what your "pictures" are, to help sort out differences between the way we imagine things are "supposed" to be and the way they really are.*

**A picture is an image or idea of the "way things are" or the "way things ought to be."** They are often simplifications, generalizations, or stereotypes, but they are still powerful. My picture of a family is a Caucasian man and woman in their early thirties with two blond children, preferably one boy and one girl. My picture of God is an old man in the clouds with a long white beard. My picture of a corporation is a faceless, heartless machine.

> • • • • • • • • •
>
> **My picture of God is an old man in the clouds with a long white beard. My picture of a corporation is a faceless, heartless machine.**

We may have pictures even when we know better—even when we have plenty of evidence that contradicts them. My picture of a minister is a middle-aged to older man in a black robe, even though I know many ministers who don't fit that description at all.

**A picture may be the first thing that comes to mind when we think of one subject or another.** What is the first thing that comes to mind when you hear the word "circus"? A picture could be a stereotype like "blondes are not very bright" or "smart people wear glasses."

Pictures also include traditions or common practices. We have pictures about proper ways to behave in certain situations and how we should be dressed. How would you react to someone who comes to a picnic in a tuxedo? What should a wedding look like?

We each have many pictures, some of which we probably confuse with reality. Can you identify any of your own pictures on subjects that are mentioned above? What pictures do you have of accountants, childhood, high school, attractiveness, fanatics, parties, muggers, funerals, sin, heaven, holidays? **What images first come to mind when you hear any one of these words?** How do they compare with what you know from direct experience? Can you trace where these images have come from?

**R E S U L T S**    *"Pictures" can have a big influence on our experience. They represent certain expectations about "the way things are supposed to be," which is often quite different than the way they really are. To look beyond our pictures takes us a step closer to the truth about our own experience. To be able to identify our pictures will help us sort out external information from our own. To look beyond pictures may help us have something new for ourselves that we couldn't imagine before.*

• • • • • • • • • • • • • • • • • • • • • •

*I am sure that when I was young I was slowly but surely taught not to cry. I don't remember specific messages, but I assume that the reason I haven't cried much over the years is the subtle or direct messages I picked up from family, friends, or the media.*

*Interestingly, art makes me cry more often than life—usually movies, like **West Side Story**, or **ET**, sometimes television. I have been moved to tears by certain McDonald's commercials, and I am sure that my emotional reaction to the 1996 Summer Olympics had much to do with the way it was presented on television.*

*I can recognize several levels of reaction, from subtle internal shifts like watery waves, to a tightening of places in my head and throat, to tears gathering in the corners of my eyes, to out and out crying (a rare occurrence, but it does happen.) At the same time I recognize my own control over these reactions, and I make decisions about displaying them, especially in public.*

*I don't really believe in the concept of sentimentality. I figure it is a label we use when we are moved by something and are embarrassed about it, or we are embarrassed because we aren't moved. In either case, to describe something as "sentimental" relieves us of the responsibility of having either our embarrassment or our tears.*

*Being moved is one of those wonderfully complex body experiences—it feels good to cry. I don't ever expect to be able to explain that one. I'm just going to "have" it even if it only happens rarely.*

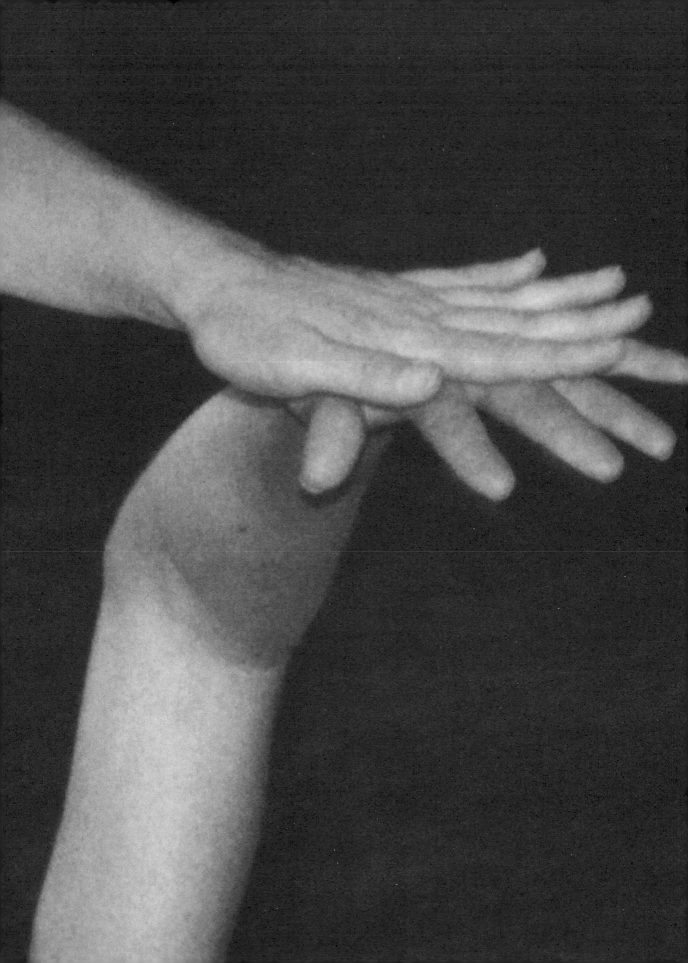

# Do We Really Share the Same Experience?

**ADVICE**   *To be aware of how "common understandings" work—the ways in which we presume that we share similar experience—will help you claim your own experience.*

**A "common understanding" is when we presume that an experience we have matches that of someone else based on our own observations or others' descriptions.**

I know when I am angry and recognize when others are angry, but if I tried to describe the physical experience of anger, I might have trouble. I didn't learn to recognize anger in myself by definition. Chances are when I was young, I or someone else behaved in a certain way and someone labeled it as "anger." Even if we can't define anger, we presume among us a common understanding of this experience.

Much of our experience is hard to define, yet we are confident that we can identify these experiences in ourselves and we believe that others share our experience.

**To presume common understandings can be both helpful and dangerous.**

Since we can't know precisely what someone else is experiencing, their inner information may really be quite different from our own. My experience of "vertigo" might involve a little dizziness. You might experience intense fear.

We may learn the name of a category before we actually

experience it. "Love," for example, is a word we probably heard before we knew about it from within. There are probably as many different ideas and experiences of love as there are people. As adults, we may still be trying to match our experience of love with what we presume others' experience to be.

If we lack precise definitions of an experience (which is usually the case), our common understandings may be largely influenced by our pictures. "Spirituality" is a huge, hard-to-define category of experience. There are also many pictures that are attached to it—white, "floaty," quiet, disembodied pictures. Are we really talking about the same thing when we talk about spirit?

> • • • • • • • • •
> **We begin to pick up some common understandings when we are very young. We are taught simplifications that may not be updated as we get older.**

We begin to pick up some common understandings when we are very young. We are taught simplifications that may not be updated as we get older. The way complex experiences or situations like death, childbirth, divorce, or war were explained to us as children may actually be quite different from the way we experience it as adults. Yet we may still carry some part of what we learned when we were young.

Much of the experience that we find difficult to objectively define is controlled or shaped by common understandings. **In order to responsibly shape our own lives, it is important for us to notice how our own experience compares to common understandings.**

Since much of our experience is difficult to articulate, we may rely on our ability to identify similarities between our own experience and others' descriptions of their experience. We presume that we are experiencing the same thing. These common understandings may also be distorted by media depictions.

........

**40**

For example, we may have a sense of what the experience of "grief" is—a presumed common understanding. But what if someone close to me dies? Do I have assumptions about the way I should react? What if I don't feel certain expected feelings or behave in expected ways? What if the process seems to last longer than others have led me to believe it would? What if I am still grieving two years later? Five years? Ten years? Can I sort out the reality of my own experience from the common understandings that I carry with me?

Don't be surprised when your actual experience is different from "common understandings." We don't tend to talk much about it among ourselves, so we have no way of knowing how very different or similar our experience is from others. Any category of experience that is controlled by common understandings is likely to be much more complex than we presume.

**R E S U L T S**  *The more we can identify and claim our own experience, the more clear we can be about what we want from life. This clarity also gives us more appreciation of the differences between us and how we can honor or mediate different or conflicting desires.*

• • • • • • • • • • • • • • • • • • • • • •

*Fear is not one experience, but many. If someone were to say to me, "I am afraid," I would only have some vague clues about what they were experiencing. I couldn't really tell very much without either observing their behavior or asking them questions to find out more information. I don't really know if someone else's fear is the same as mine, especially since I experience so many different kinds of fear.*

*Don't expect me to do any serious rock climbing with you. Too scary. Just watching it on television is almost too much. Even those steeply raked sports stadiums concern me (I have a recurring nightmare about tumbling from the higher seats), but I do still attend an occasional basketball game. The roller coaster at Great America is scary, but fun. The ride where you drop straight down several stories in a little cage is also fun, but creates enough fear in me that the wait in line can be a challenge. I remember being extremely nervous before performing in musicals in high school, but I still chose to do it. Now when I perform I don't get nearly so nervous, and the level of fear that I experience has that exciting adrenaline–soaked quality. The first time I recite something from memory it is very frightening. After that, though, it isn't very scary at all. Entering large social groups for the first time (or anytime for that matter) is daunting. Is that fear? I am always a little concerned about getting feedback about anything I have created. Is that fear, too?*

*I realize that I'm not always sure how to name my own experience. Why should I presume that I understand what anyone else is experiencing?*

# Our Lives Are Full of Splits

**A D V I C E** *Identify the splits in your life: it is the first step toward healing them.*

**The splits between body, mind, heart, and spirit are only part of the problem. Our lives are full of splits, including ones that are reinforced by culture and language.** We are asked to view the world and our experience of it as a collection of independent, if not conflicting, parts rather than seeing it as a whole.

From birth we are taught to separate, divide, categorize, fragment, and polarize. The words we are given, the institutions that have been created, the philosophies and theologies that we have been taught are full of splits.

Some splits are large, some are small. Some are easy to heal, others will take time and energy. Some are personal, but others are deeply ingrained in the culture. Some splits are too difficult to change—we'll work around those.

Here are some examples of splits:

- We have splits between what we know deep inside and what we are willing to admit. If we have experience that seems abnormal or unacceptable, we may go to great lengths to hide that knowledge from others and even deny it ourselves.

- We experience splits in the ways we behave in different situations. For example, we act one way at work and another when we are with friends. We may play very different "roles" in different situations.

- We experience the split of peer pressure when we

........

**43**

struggle between what we want and what the group demands of us.

- We split up into racial and ethnic groups and different religious denominations and faiths.

- We split work and play into two completely separate categories.

- We experience splits between seemingly contradictory experiences in our own bodies—the desire to be alone and the need for community, a need for both control and letting go of control, or wanting attention and shrinking from it.

- We have splits in our political system between liberals and conservatives, Republicans and Democrats. Even though our personal philosophies may be quite varied, actually integrating wide points of view, the system encourages polarization and distrust. We become reactionary and defensive in response to other opinions.

- We split our corporations and organizations into parts that rarely communicate with each other, parts that compete rather than cooperate.

What are the splits that you see in your own life or in the world around you? What changes would you like to make to experience more wholeness in your life?

Do you feel cut off from some part of your experience? Is there something you want that you are not getting?

Are there people from whom you are separated or estranged? Are there situations that force you to hide part of who you are?

Are there areas of conflict in your life? Are these due to some sort of split?

Are there political, ideological, religious, or racial splits in your community? Do you experience your country as being split politically?

Are you separated from spiritual or religious experience, or do you experience splits in your faith community?

Are there parts of yourself that you find difficult to admit to yourself or others?

Does your family, community, or culture ask you to be a certain way that you find uncomfortable?

It can be challenging, even painful, to focus on the splits in our lives. But to realize that there are splits, and even that we are encouraged to be split in many situations, is important.

**To recognize splits and articulate them to ourselves and others is often the biggest step we can make toward healing them.**

• • • • • • • • •
We experience splits between seemingly contradictory experiences in our own bodies—the desire to be alone and the need for community, a need both for control and being out of control, or wanting attention and shrinking from it.

To realize that there are splits also lets us know that wholeness is possible. If we can name a split, we can take the first step toward healing it, even if it is only a small one.

**RESULTS**   *Wholeness and integration are much more possible when we acknowledge our splits. The bits and pieces of our lives can be brought together like the multicolored threads of a tapestry.*

• • • • • • • •

• • • • • • • • • • • • • • • • • • • • •

*I have a nice, serviceable car. Older, functional, easy to maintain, and inexpensive as cars go. I know darn well that cars aren't important status symbols to me. If I am going to throw around my disposable income, I will buy a computer gadget or two, which will not only increase my productivity and creativity, but in certain circles also has status value—especially when people find out I really know how to use them!*

*Despite the authority and solidity of my inner "car" information, I still feel the desire more often than I care to admit to have a snazzy late model something–or–other, preferably red. When the commercials appear on television, I find myself whining to my partner, "I wanna Lexus."*

*I know this is a split. It may be a minor one on the cosmic scale, but it is clear to me that I am never going to completely resolve it. I blame it alternately on commercial television (and even PBS has an occasional car endorsement these days), the American obsession with automobiles, and vestiges of midlife crisis—my own and others!*

# Thinking and Talking Splits

**A D V I C E**  *Language shapes our experience. Notice how the way we talk and the way we think actually creates or encourages splits.*

The language and ideas we are taught as we grow up are full of splits. If we use split language and split ideas, then we are likely to experience fragmentation in our lives. The way I "see" something will have a big effect on my experience.

Let's look at this relationship between ideas and experience.

**A construct is way of looking at or thinking about something—a system for understanding or describing some aspect of reality.** Constructs are not the same as reality, although constructs have a very large effect on the way we experience reality.

For example, we have a system for organizing time: minutes, hours, days, weeks, months, years. This is a construct. Different cultures have used different calendars and systems to describe the reality of time. Although we may believe that we have the best or most accurate method for organizing time, it is not the only one that has ever been used, nor will it go unchanged in the future.

Constructs are powerful shapers of reality. Days, weeks, and months are very real to us. "Happy New Year! Let's make resolutions." "Oh God, I'm forty years old!" "It's Monday morning. Back to work!" Our constructs may not always match our experience, however. In our construct of time, the seconds, minutes, and hours tick by very regularly, at the same constant speed. Our experience of time is different: sometimes it seems to pass by very slowly and other times very quickly.

As we acquire language, we acquire constructs as well, like the time construct or ones that have to do with family, love, government, social status, home, even how we drive from one place to another.

We take constructs for granted, even if they conflict with our experience. We accept current ideas about "family" even if our own family experience is completely different.

**The way we divide our experience into the categories of "mind," "heart," "body," and "spirit" is one of these language/idea splits.** There are other ways we define our experience, but this one is pervasive. We are taught from early on that we can take the bits and pieces of our lives and consign them to different categories. In the process we are discouraged from seeing how our experience is completely intertwined. We are cheated out of wholeness.

To shift our language and our ways of thinking are important steps toward healing splits. If I see the American political scene as a wide and fluid range of political points of view, I will have a completely different experience than if I believe that it is divided into two clearly defined competing camps. If I define "body" and "spirit" as two completely different categories of experience, I will have difficulty integrating them in my life.

Shifting our language, ways of thinking, or actions takes practice. But through this practice we can decrease the splits in our lives.

> • • • • • • • • •
> **Shifting our language, ways of thinking, or actions takes practice. But through this practice we can decrease the splits in our lives.**

**RESULTS** *More and more you will notice how language and cultural constructs contain splits. This will make it easier to shift the way you talk and think in ways that will encourage wholeness.*

• • • • • • • • • • • • • • • • • • • • • •

I am on a crusade against "continuums." We are fond of drawing lines between two "polar opposites" as a way of depicting two extremes and a range of variations between them: good and evil, liberal and conservative, gay and straight, pro–choice and pro–life, happy and sad.

Continuums encourage "split" thinking. They demand that I perch at one and only one point on the line. But what if I am a fiscal conservative and a social liberal, or what if I can see the truth in aspects of both pro–choice and pro–life arguments, or what if I am capable of having tears and laughter at the same time? The simplistic geometry of a straight line stiffly holding apart two opposing ends can't depict that experience.

Continuums are easy to visualize, but they fail to describe the complexity of our beliefs or experience. Perhaps we need circles, spirals, cobwebs, or cubes as our "maps." Perhaps we need to practice "having" and letting be the seeming contradictions in our experience. We contain both good and evil, liberal and conservative, happy and sad at the very same time.

# It's Happening All at the Same Time

**ADVICE** *Notice that many things are going on in your physical experience at the same time. Realize that you can't pay attention to more than one at a time, but that a lot is happening nonetheless.*

Do you drive a car, perhaps with a stick shift? If you do, have you noticed how you can work the foot pedals, control the steering wheel, windshield wipers, and headlights, check both the rearview mirrors, judge the curve in the road, fiddle with the radio, carry on a conversation, be on the lookout for police cars, think to yourself, discipline the kids in the backseat, and curse the occasional bad driver, all in an overlapping fashion?

**We each have layers and layers of constant and simultaneous experience:** thoughts, feelings, memories, sensations, insights, movements, reactions, impulses, discomforts, and pleasures. We can only pay attention to one or a few of them in a short period of time, but our bodyspirits are quite capable of doing, having, and holding a lot in each moment.

........

**51**

We get in trouble when we deny this reality rather than taking advantage of it. One of the reasons we have "splits" is because we try to analyze, separate, and categorize these layers of integrated and interwoven experience.

We often use the term "bodyspirit" to describe the integrated nature of our experience. Each of us is unique. Look around a crowded room sometime. Isn't it apparent that each of us is different, and that this is the expression of our "spirit?"

We are each complex and complicated. If we pick apart the various aspects of who we are, we may find seeming contradictions, but our bodyspirits hold them all.

We are amazed by "paradoxes." How can two seeming contradictions both be true? Our bodyspirits don't have any problem claiming both, but *thinking* about this reality can be a challenge. "Let go of control in order to gain it?"—hard to understand conceptually, but considerably easier to "know."

> • • • • • • • • •
> **If I think about all the roles I play—son, artist, partner, dancer, leader, friend, writer, lover, organizer, bookkeeper, singer, preacher—I get exhausted. But my bodyspirit contains them with ease.**

Sometimes when we are "confused," we are, in fact, muddled. But other times I believe we are experiencing the body's ability to include several realities at once, even if they seem to be in conflict.

If I think about all the roles I play—son, artist, partner, dancer, leader, friend, writer, lover, organizer, bookkeeper, singer, preacher—I get exhausted. But my bodyspirit contains them with ease.

What do you do with this information, this amazing bodyspirit ability? Relax! Don't try to figure it out, just enjoy it. Breathe rather than analyze. Embrace paradox, contradiction, and even confusion. Have tears and laughter at the same time, or community and loneliness, or hope and fear, or liberal and conservative. Don't try to split them apart.

**RESULTS** *To recognize the bodyspirit's ability to have several things going on at once even if we can't pay attention to*

*all of them is a wonderful way to bring the parts of ourselves back into a whole. We can just let them "be" together.*

• • • • • • • • • • • • • • • • • • • • • •

*One morning as I sat writing, it dawned on me to try an experiment: could I describe the physical experiences I was having right at that moment?*

*This is what I noticed:*

> It is mid–morning and I have been up since 7:30. I am pretty much awake, but I still feel the "morningness" in my eyes. I don't have my contact lens on—my glasses mildly annoy me. I've not showered yet. I often work for a few hours before I do. I like this pattern of working, but it also seems like the day hasn't fully begun.
>
> I have only had two pieces of toast and a glass of milk to eat so far. I'm not hungry but not satisfied either.
>
> I am doing some writing. It stimulates me, but it is also a struggle. I fight the urge to get up and move around to release the extra energy and stretch my legs.
>
> I wonder where this piece will end up...will it make sense? Will it get any attention? Will *I* get any attention? I know that if I read through it now it will seem disjointed and incomplete. That would be frustrating.
>
> I'm sitting on the couch working on a laptop. My position hasn't changed much for a while. I feel the weight of the  computer on my thighs. My legs are crossed at the ankle and my calves are clammy where they touch. I'm not sitting up straight, but my back doesn't hurt, thank God. I should sit up straight anyway. The radiant heater hanging from the ceiling of my loft makes me too warm. My discomfort is less compelling than the writing, however, so I keep working. I give myself credit for perseverance.
>
> Even as I write, I think about plans for the rest of the day...images from the dance concert I saw the previous evening float through my mind...I worry about a current

design job that has hit a snag (but I am not as anxious as I was on Tuesday when the problem cropped up.)

*All this was happening in a brief moment. It only took a minute or two to take notes on what was going on, but it took over an hour to describe it in a readable form.*

*We don't need to keep track of everything. Most of it will keep rolling along without us getting too focused on it.*

# "Focus" Less & "Have" More

**ADVICE**  *Learn the difference between "focusing" and "having." See if you can increase the amount of "having" in your life.*

When I focus with my eyes, I can clearly see only one small area at a time. As I look at a crowd of people, for example, only one face will be clear, even though I may see others in my peripheral vision. Something similar happens when I "notice" my experience, or when I recall or imagine something. I only focus on one piece at a time.

To focus is to examine one thread in a large tapestry, to pick out the sound of a clarinet in a symphony orchestra, to taste the cilantro in a mixed green salad.

**"Having" on the other hand is taking in a whole experience, realizing that many things are going on in our bodyspirits at one time, and enjoying or savoring that experience.** To have is to enjoy the rich, multilayered quality of the tapestry, the symphony, or the green salad.

In our culture, which strives so mightily to be rational, there is a high value placed on focusing. We analyze, judge, critique, and seek explanations. We are not encouraged to enjoy, or to indulge, except by those who want us to buy their products. So we take the tapestry and rip it apart into tiny shreds in a pile on the floor before we have even had a chance to see it as whole, we criticize the clarinet player rather than savoring the multitude of other sounds the orchestra has to offer, and we push the salad aside rather than eating around the cilantro.

Focusing is not a bad thing. It is good to be able to pay

attention to the bits and pieces of our experience. But **we definitely lack balance between focusing and having**. Notice for yourself: Are you encouraged to critique or enjoy? Can you claim the good parts of an experience, or do you let the negative parts spoil the whole thing? Do you celebrate your strengths, or do you dwell on your weaknesses? After a performance, do you itemize the things you disliked or the ones you liked?

**We invite you to look at the world with an "easy" focus.** Try this experiment: furrow your brow and stare at something intensely across the room. Look at yourself in the mirror with

• • • • • • • • •
In our culture, which strives so mightily to be rational, there is a high value placed on focusing. We analyze, judge, critique, and seek explanations.

the same expression. What do you see? How does this expression feel in your body? Now close your eyes, take a deep breath or two, and then open your eyes again and take in the whole scene, regardless of what you are looking at, in a more relaxed way. Enjoy what you see. Take it in as a gift. Look for the good, look for what pleases you. Think of it as eating dessert with your eyes. This is "easy" focus, and to practice it will increase the amount of "having" in your life.

We have a great deal of control over how we take in the world. You have a clear choice: you can look at it and criticize, fret, and obsess. Or you can savor and enjoy. **By practicing "having" rather than "focusing," by looking for the good rather than fixing on the problems, you can be noticeably happier and healthier.** You will find that you have more energy in your life. Often problems can become non–problems just by shifting from "focusing" to "having."

It does take practice to "have" more. If you are a life–long focuser, it may require lots of practice. But take it one step at a time. Look for what you like—enjoy it and take it in. Comment on it to yourself or to another. When critical messages come to you, let them pass by. Keep them to yourself, rather than sharing them with others, despite how tempting it may be to do so. If you find yourself focusing on a problem, see if you can look around it to see what is good or pleasing.

**To "have" rather than "focus" is not a process of denial.** It doesn't absolve us of our responsibility to solve the problems that face us. And "focusing" can be positive and powerful. What our bodies need, however, is more balance between focusing and having. As a culture we are far too focused on focusing.

**The easiest way to shift from focusing to having is to take a deep breath.** Sigh, if you aren't embarrassed to make some noise. Shake all or part of your body. Close your eyes and relax your brow and your jaw. These are all simple ways of "having."

**RESULTS** *To increase "having" in your life will increase your sense of satisfaction. To be able to have an "easy" focus will give you another way of seeing the world, one with more ease and appreciation.*

• • • • • • • • • • • • • • • • • • • • • •

*It has made such a difference in my life to practice not judging. Instead of critiquing everything and everyone I come in contact with I look for the good, no matter how much or how little there is. The critical voices are still there, I just pay less attention to them. I call those inner messages "static." I no longer cling to my "static."*

*Two amazing things have come out of this practice. The first is that I have learned that it is not the job of the world, or any of its institutions, structures, or people to be or do just what I want. Neither my family nor workplace nor church nor best friends are here on earth just to serve my wants and needs. They are a gift from which I can draw goodness.*

*I have greatly reduced my expectations. As a result I am disappointed less often and my level of appreciation has skyrocketed.*

*The other amazing thing is that as I practice judging others less, I judge myself less. What a relief! I have been giving myself a big break. The result is that I feel much more creative, generous, and satisfied.*

*What a concept: less–conditional (if not unconditional) love for myself, others, and the world!*

# Having Spirit in Our Lives

**A D V I C E**  *To claim spirit information in our personal and community lives may be difficult in our culture. But regardless of whether you are part of a particular religious tradition or can articulate a specific theology, you can "have" your spirit information.*

**"Spirit" demands some special attention.** It may be the most difficult part of the mind/body/heart/spirit construct to deal with. It seems to be walled off from the rest of our experience. There is a deep split for us here both individually and as a community or culture. In order to reintegrate it into the whole, we will need to look at it more directly.

> • • • • • • • • •
> We fear that if we begin a discussion about God, we will end up in an argument or a standoff, so we avoid the discussion to begin with.

**Why is it difficult to discuss spirit issues in our culture? Where do we feel free to discuss this part of our experience? What can we do to make it easier?**

Are spirit issues the same as theology? Do we have to believe in God in order to claim spirit issues? If we are not involved in a religious tradition, can we still "have" our spirit information?

What are our "pictures" about spirit? How can we shift our pictures about body and spirit so that they don't need to be separate?

Can we redefine what spiritual disciplines are?

**Our lack of freedom surrounding spirit issues keeps us from integrating that experience into the whole of our lives.** We can notice and claim more of our spirit information with practice and with tools.

**It is difficult in our culture to discuss or define spirit information. It is wrapped in and around theology and religion, which we are uncomfortable dealing with in the secular world.**

Some people go to church or mosque or synagogue, some don't. Some believe in God, some don't. The ones who do don't always agree with each other. Some people grew up in a religious tradition but have rejected it or drifted away. Others have rediscovered religion with various levels of zeal. Others have found deep meaning in alternative practices, either new or old.

Public discussion about religion is hampered by our political system which separates church and state. Is it acceptable to include religion in the public sphere, or is it a violation of the Constitution? The irony is that despite this separation, religion and politics are completely enmeshed, often in frustrating ways.

We fear that if we begin a discussion about God, we will end up in an argument or a standoff, so we avoid the discussion altogether. Unfortunately in the process we also cut ourselves off from a whole range of experience that is both important and accessible. **This range of experience includes issues like connection, affirmation, community, suffering, truth, hospitality, forgiveness, commitment, inclusion, friendship, love, transcendence, family, reconciliation, life, death, justice, gratitude, communion, balance, mystery, interdependence, solidarity, awe, power, service, sacrifice, home, grace, humility, hope, and trust.**

These issues are woven in and around our lives—we know them instantly. We must reclaim our ability to "have" them.

Spirit is ultimately experiential rather than philosophical. We can have this information even if we can't articulate a personal theology. **One of the first steps in reclaiming spirit information is to change the way we discuss it.** Rather than starting on the theological roof—"What is God?"—we can begin with the foundation: What are the details of our own experience? Look at the list above—connection, affirmation, community…trust—these are all issues we share regardless of our theological stance or practice. They are part of our daily lives, our direct experience.

How can we begin to discuss these issues for our own benefit and the benefit of the community? We might begin by asking some questions of ourselves and others that will elicit our own information on a particular subject.

For example, "suffering" is a spirit issue. Here are some questions we might ask about our experience with pain and suffering:

- Have I experienced intense pain or difficulty of any sort (mind, body, heart, spirit)?

- Have there been extended periods of time that I have been in pain?

- When have I been with others who have been in intense pain or difficulty?

- How much pain am I willing to endure?

- What have I been taught about enduring pain?

- How have I dealt with eliminating pain and suffering in my own life?

- How have I helped eliminate the pain and suffering of others either directly or indirectly?

- What do I "think" or "believe" works to reduce the suffering of others?

- Do I actually do these things myself?

- How do I feel about my own or others' use of drugs or alcohol to reduce pain and suffering?

- Have I ever considered suicide to end my own suffering?

- Have I ever wished that someone else could die to end their suffering?

These are all body wisdom questions directly related to our own experience. We could ask specific questions about any of the issues in the list above. We can approach these issues in a way that is personal and concrete, rather than distant or hypothetical.

**Spirit information is physical.** It is not separate from our bodies, it *is* our bodies. It is both ordinary and extraordinary. It is both simple and profound. It is something to "have" rather than something to "know." It is part of our individual life and our community life as well.

Let me give you some examples of the way in which the issues of our lives are surrounded by spirit information:

1. The way we live our lives is becoming more and more fragmented. The neighborhood is no longer the center of community for us. We travel great distances to work, play, educate and entertain our children, worship, eat. The neighborhood used to fulfill certain "spirit" functions that it may no longer perform, having to do with home, belonging, safety, mutual support, familiarity of place, being known, friendship, companionship, interconnection. We spend a great deal of time at work, but can the workplace serve as community? Do we even consider it appropriate to raise these issues in the workplace?

2. As a culture, we face more and more questions about medical care and "quality of life." We are being given more information and more choice in our treatment and care, including decisions about when and how we will die. These choices are sometimes in conflict with the plans or desires of doctors and other healthcare providers. Spirit issues surround this debate—mortality and immortality, suffering, family, home, comfort,

care, autonomy and control, being with loved ones, the sanctity of life. The medical community is not always willing or prepared to include these issues, but they are a crucial part of our well–being and need to be included in medical debates.

3. There is a general fear in our culture right now about employment. "Downsizing," layoffs, and plant closures create an uneasiness among us, even though the rate of unemployment is low. These spirit issues are woven into this concern: community, friendship, stability, security, loyalty, sharing, sacrifice, mutuality, and justice.

Spirit flows beyond religious institutions. It is not isolated to certain times or places. It is not separate from our bodies, nor is it separate from minds or hearts. **It is important to recognize, however, that we have been separated from our spirit information.** We can reclaim it. To include spirit information in our personal and corporate lives is to heal splits. It is to reintegrate and to "have" all of our information.

### How can we do this?

The first step in reclaiming our spirit information is to recognize that it is a difficult subject to deal with in our culture. Next, we can recognize that spirit issues include a broad range of subjects that are directly related to our everyday lives. Finally, if we approach these issues from the point of view of our own experience, gathering our own body wisdom and that of others, we may avoid the contentiousness of theological or philosophical debate.

**R E S U L T S**  *Being able to have our spirit information is an important part of being whole. We can also have a new appreciation of how spirit issues are woven into all aspects of our lives.*

• • • • • • • • • • • • • • • • • • • • • • •

*One of my desires is to have spirit in my life all or most of the time. It has never been enough just to get it on Sunday morning, so I have been trying to suffuse my whole life with it. Although I have been pretty successful with this, there are still areas of my life in which having spirit is a challenge.*

*In my work, I have to do a fair amount of administration—keeping records, paying bills, dealing with details on one project or twenty. My previous approach to this task was firmly based in an efficiency model. Let's plow through this stack of papers with alacrity! I am actually quite good at that. I can be very focused and productive. But I have noticed recently that it also leaves me breathless.*

*I have been trying to slow down the pace a bit so I can administrate and breathe at the same time—imagine paying the bills with a "lying in a hammock" kind of attitude. Frankly, at this point it is driving me a little crazy. Half of me is practicing the art of Zen stamp–licking, while the inner voices are screeching, "Get this done, and get it done now!!"*

*I fully expect to get better at this with practice.*

# Explode Your Spirit "Pictures"

 **A D V I C E** *If you have certain "pictures" about spirit, these may get in the way of actually "having" spirit. Sort out your spirit pictures from your actual experience. Claim and enjoy your spirit information.*

**It is important that we not be controlled by our spirit "pictures."** Remember that a "picture" is an internal idea or image of the way things are or the way things are supposed to be. Pictures may seem to be part of our internal experience but have actually come from external sources.

These are the spirit pictures that I have picked up, or have heard others express:

- the spirit is separate from the body

- the body is merely a vessel or container for the spirit

- spirit is good and the body is evil

- spirit is ethereal—white, "floaty," disembodied, "up there"

- spirituality only happens at church, synagogue, or mosque

- spirituality only occurs when we are being quiet, still, and contained

- spirituality means being serious and somber

- discussion of spirituality isn't appropriate in many secular settings

- spirituality speaks in a whisper

- spirituality is primarily a solitary affair

My picture of a spiritual person is someone who is very calm and serene, never moves very quickly or talks too loudly, never gets angry, sits still a lot, smiles knowingly but doesn't laugh very much, never tells politically incorrect jokes, doesn't have sex, prays or contemplates often if not constantly, is never petty, jealous, vengeful, or greedy, says wise things, doesn't have a real job except perhaps helping the poor which he or she would do for free, has a relationship with God that I could never hope to match, spends a lot of time alone, and probably isn't very young or attractive.

> • • • • • • • • •
> **We believe that "spirit" is a physical experience. Even though it may seem to be larger than us, or outside of us, we would not be able to recognize or identify spiritual experience unless there were something going on in our bodies.**

**Any part of a picture may be partially true, but it is important to sort out what isn't.** It is also important to be able to reclaim information that might be excluded by our pictures. For example, we may have been taught that it is important or even "required" to be married. There are many good reasons to be married, but if, for example, we never find the right partner, this should not keep us from finding happiness as a single person.

Here are some of the ways that we can shift "spirit" pictures:

• **"Spirit" may include but is not limited to our relationship with a higher power.** It also includes a whole range of issues listed in the previous chapter that most everyone experiences to one extent or another whether they believe in God or not.

• **We believe that "spirit" is a physical experience.** Even though it may seem to be larger than us, or outside of us, we would not be able to recognize or identify spiritual experience unless there were something going on in our bodies. This means that body and spirit are not separate at all, but are actually completely intertwined if not inseparable. We need our bodies to have spirit.

- **We recognize that "spirit" can happen anywhere and anytime, not just in the midst of religious practice.** We can have spirit information during all sorts of activities: dancing, laughing, making love, running, singing, playing, hiking, taking a shower, cuddling, working, doing the dishes, eating, and many more. It may be precisely these activities that create spirit experience for us.

- **Spirit is not really separate from any other part of our experience.** Spirit issues are also body issues, mind issues, and heart issues. If we see them as integrated into our whole lives, rather than being set apart, we will more likely experience wholeness.

- **Spirituality may be individual, but it is also occurs in relationship and in community.**

- **Spirit experience occurs in activity as well as in stillness and quiet.**

 **RESULTS**    *With practice we can learn to trust our own inner authority about spiritual experience—what is currently true for us. Although religious tradition and leadership may be one of the most difficult forms of external authority to question, it is possible. It may even lead to a truer, deeper, and more enlivening spirituality.*

........

**70**

•••••••••••••••••••••

*I have a suspicion that God and Santa were twins separated at birth. They are both older men with long white beards, they both live "up" somewhere, they both know when you are sleeping and when you are awake, and whether you have been bad or* good. (So you know what you better be doing, for goodness sake!) They are both generous in their gift giving, but pretty much rely on us to do the actual legwork.

This idea was confirmed by Cynthia's daughter, Katie. When Katie was about three she went through a phase where she was fascinated and a little frightened by Santa. For her, anyone with a long white beard (at any time of the year) was Santa. Our performing company musician, Amar, has a long white and grey beard, and when Katie saw him, perhaps for the first time, she said "Santa!"

One day, Katie was over at my house and she wanted to look through a large picture book I had about the artwork of Michaelango. Of course there are many God images in the book— also older men with long white beards. Every time we turned the page and there was another of these images, she would say "Santa!" At one point, I turned the page and there was a scowling God. Katie said with a sense of awe, "Santa angry."

I don't know what pictures Katie will grow up with about God, but chances are they will be similar to mine—older guy with white beard and booming voice. Or maybe she will end up with lots of different pictures. I hope so. Meanwhile, I'll just keep on trying to shift my own.

# Grace Is Physical

**ADVICE** *By noticing what creates the physical experience of grace for you, you can heal the split between body and spirit and create a life with more energy and abundance for you and others.*

Over a period of years, we have asked groups of people that we have led to call out words that describe the experience they have in their bodies when they are in stress. The words pour out effortlessly: tense, constricted, harried, nervous, closed, pressured, tired, confused, tight, and so on. **Although people may have slightly different ways of describing stress, almost everyone seems to be able to identify the experience in their bodies.** We are very aware of stress in our culture, aren't we? We talk about it often, and there is a widespread cultural agreement that we should be reducing it.

But when we reduce stress are we merely returning to some neutral state—the absence of these physical symptoms?

**What if we were to ask people to describe the physical experience that is the opposite of stress?** We have done this, and these sorts of words emerge: open, relaxed, breathing, calm, peaceful, satisfied, generous, energized, creative, and so on. We have chosen to give this experience a name. We call it the "physicality of grace."

Grace is a church word with a long history. But it is still a murky concept for many, even those brought up in the church. Rather than approaching grace from the cosmic end of the scale, we have chosen to see how it works in individual and corporate bodies.

**Most people report that they can identify this physical experience that we have named "grace."** Even though it may vary from person to person, virtually all of the people we have asked claim this ability. *This is body data*, or experience in the moment.

**If we are able to identify grace in the moment, then we may, over time, be able to recognize that it tends to occur in some places more than others, with certain people, in the midst of certain activities.** Where are you, what are you doing, who are you with when you have this experience? When we ask groups this question, the answers are rich and varied: being in nature, working in the garden, listening to music, being with friends, playing with grandchildren, singing, taking a shower or a long bath, taking walks, jogging, or swimming. and many others. *This is body knowledge.*

> ● ● ● ● ● ● ● ● ●
> Rather than approaching grace from the cosmic end of the scale, we have chosen to see how it works in individual and corporate bodies.

If you can recognize the experience of grace in the moment, and if you can also notice when it tends to occur for you, then you should be able, with this information, to create more grace in your life. Doesn't this make sense? You can choose to be in these situations more often—to be with the people who enrich your life, to engage in the activities that give you energy, to go to the places that feed your soul. **You can make it a point to have more grace. You don't have to wait until it mysteriously happens.** *This is body wisdom.*

Here is some other "grace" body wisdom:

- **Stress takes its toll on our bodies.** It has both short–term and long–term negative effects. Even though it may stimulate us to high levels of creativity or productivity in the short term, our bodies rebel if we stay in this state for too long. **In contrast, grace has long–term positive physical effects.** We are convinced that besides the immediate satisfaction of the experience of grace—its sheer pleasure—there are benefits to our ongoing health and wholeness from having grace in our lives. The more we have it, the better off we will be.

- **Stress and grace affect not only our own bodies, but those around us as well.** Have you noticed what it is like to live or work with someone who is in stress? It affects you too, doesn't it? If I am in stress, I must be communicating that experience to others. In contrast, if I am around "grace–full" people, it has a positive affect on me. If I am experiencing grace, won't that be communicated to others? Notice the people around you. Who is "giving off" stress? Who is emanating grace? What are you putting out into the world? Stress begets stress. Grace begets grace.

- **As human beings, we are all grace–makers.** There have been many times when other people have created grace in my life. I would presume from this that I have also created grace for others at times. This may be hard to claim if we carry with us religious teachings about the nature of God and grace. This may also be hard to claim if we have been taught to avoid taking credit for anything out of a sense of real or false humility. But again notice—are there people either near you or far away who have created grace for you through specific words or actions? What was it that they did? What have you done recently to create grace for someone either directly or indirectly? What sorts of things might you do to create grace for someone else?

- **Artists are often grace–makers.** There may be people who are not directly in our lives but who have created grace for us and others through artistic creations: songs, dances, poems, stories, comedy routines, symphonies, essays, prayers, sermons, visual art, photographs. These and other artistic creations are powerful vehicles for making grace and have the potential for widening the circle of grace. What artists have been grace–makers for you?

- **There are little grace experiences and big grace experiences and every size and shape in between.** When I take a deep breath and let it out with a sigh, I immediately get at least a small sense of grace. Sometimes grace is as big as feeling at one with the entire universe. But the experience of grace need not be a great epiphany or mountain–top experience. It can be quite immediate and common.

To look at grace from the point of view of physicality does not keep us from pondering or celebrating its mysterious source. Frankly, I think this great pool of grace that we have access to *is* God. But that belief is clearer to me on some days than on others, and I don't want my lack of theological clarity and anyone else's question or disbelief to get in the way of us "having" grace for ourselves and creating grace for others.

 **RESULTS** *To be able to recognize and have the physicality of grace in your life is a huge gift. This new awareness will make it easy to create more grace for yourself. It will also be clearer how you create grace in other's lives and in the world.*

• • • • • • • • • • • • • • • • • • • • • •

*When they pray, some people use strings of beads to guide them through a particular series of prayers, which are repeated over and over again. Even though I have never tried it, I am sure it works. It makes sense to me that to combine a tactile experience with the repetition of certain memorized words would change my inner experience in some way, perhaps dramatically.*

*But here is my question: what if I reach this same state with actions or words that are not particularly religious? Would this still be a spiritual discipline or prayer? What if it happened to me through gardening, or walking in the woods, petting the cat, or even as I collated and stapled a whole pile of photo-copied articles?*

*Perhaps it is not my job to figure out God, but to have the God–experience however and whenever it comes to me, to take it in, to relish it, and then to move it outward in my life.*

# Big Spirit?
# Big Body!

 **ADVICE** *The idea that spirit is "big" may get in the way of reintegrating body and spirit. It helps to realize that our physicality is "big"—it extends well beyond our "edges."*

I used to have trouble with the idea that body and spirit were completely intertwined. The reason: in my pictures, "spirit" was broad and expansive while my body seemed to be quite limited. It seemed like it would be necessary to "pull in" my understanding of spirit to fit with a limited view of my physicality. Is this true for you? Do the "limits" of physicality and the "expansiveness" of spirituality make it difficult for you to integrate body and spirit?

**Over time I realized that I had another choice: I could expand my view of my physicality.** Much evidence suggests that our bodies are not bounded by the envelope of our skin. I do not end right at that edge. In very concrete ways, my physicality extends well beyond that.

Here are four examples to support this view:

- **Have you ever had the experience of someone standing just a little too close to you**—not touching but definitely in your space? **Each of us carries a kind of body territory.** It may extend out different distances for different people. It may vary from culture to culture, but we can definitely feel it, can't we? This is the first clue that our physicality is not bounded by our skin.

- **Have you ever noticed how your body reacts when someone nearby falls, or turns, or jumps?** Do you remember what it was like to watch a trapeze artist swing through the air, or a tightrope walker balance on a wire high above the ground? Have you ever gotten tired just from having children running all around you, even though you were sitting still? Have you been around someone who was depressed and you began to feel dragged down yourself? **At a deep physical level, our bodies receive and respond to the physical information, especially the movement, of other bodies. We call this body–to–body communication.** We have the experience almost as if it is happening to us. This is the effect that dancers on the stage or football players on the field have on us. This is a definite physical experience that connects us with other bodies. Our physicality extends out toward other bodies.

> • • • • • • • • •
> **I am connected physically with people in Chicago, Bloomington, Minneapolis, Seattle, Rochester, St. Louis, Sydney, Bangkok, and many other places.**

- Can you think of someone that you love that is in another part of the country or the world, even someone who has died? **Isn't that a connection that is much deeper than a thought or idea? Isn't that a physical connection that extends far out into space and even time?** I am connected physically with people in Chicago, Bloomington, Minneapolis, Seattle, Rochester, St. Louis, Sydney, Bangkok, and many other places. In many religious traditions we are called to see all people as brothers and sisters. That means that we are invited to have the same sort of connection with people we don't even know. I am connected with Sri Lanka, Ireland, Lebanon, Vietnam, and Malawi.

- **Finally, we are physically connected with anything we can see or hear.** Light and sound rays, invisible but no less real, are moving between us and objects at huge distances. On a clear night I can see the planet Mars in the sky. That means that rays of light have moved directly from that planet millions of miles away to the retina in the back of my eyeball. I am physically connected with Mars.

We could probably carry these connections farther, but here is the point: we have a choice about how we see our physicality. We can see it ending at the envelope of our skin, or we can see that it extends over great distances— even perhaps infinitely. And we can do this at the same time we understand the limitations of our bodyspirits: even though you are connected to Mars, it can still be a struggle to get out of bed in the morning.

**Yes, "spirit" is big, but so is "body."** There are many reasons for us to close this gap between body and spirit, or bodyspirit as we call it. To see it as a whole is better for our health and well–being. It is the healing of a major split.

**RESULTS**  *If you have difficulty having body and spirit together, it may be due to your "pictures." Shifting to a larger understanding of your physicality will make it easier to see body and spirit as one.*

• • • • • • • • • • • • • • • • • • • • •

*In our performances and lectures, I often find myself claiming my Midwestern Hoosier roots (I was born and raised in Indiana.) This is so that if and when I say weird things the audience will be less quick to dismiss them as typically Californian.*

*When I talk about the idea of big bodies and big spirits and mention the part about being connected to Mars by light rays it feels weird. I don't know if I am picking up something from the audience, or if my Hoosier normality detector is working too hard. At any rate, I imagine that the audience might next expect me to talk about UFO sightings.*

*However, the Mars idea, as weird as it may sound, is becoming more interesting to me as time goes on, not so much because of the Mars part, but because it reminds me of several things that we believe in but can't see: light rays, sound rays, radiation, air, ozone, and so on. We don't really consider our belief in these unseen things as an act of faith, do we? We are doing science, not theology.*

*But does that make them any less mysterious? I am completely amazed by the idea that a light ray can travel all the way from Mars to me, and that the connection is physical. I really don't care who can explain it. And I don't really care how weird it sounds!*

# Redefining Spiritual Disciplines

**ADVICE**  *Expand your pictures of what spiritual disciplines are and then find some that you want to practice. Recognize the spiritual disciplines that you are already practicing and claim that goodness.*

Since we are redefining spirit information, we can also take a new look at the meaning of "spiritual disciplines."

**If all of our experience is physical, then spiritual disciplines are also physical.** This may fly in the face of our pictures that spiritual disciplines have a lot to do with quieting, escaping, avoiding, transcending, or punishing our bodies.

This new definition of spiritual disciplines includes two criteria:

1. **Spiritual disciplines are repeated activities**—things we do over and over again, things we "practice." They are all physical.

2. **They are things we do for our own good, the good of others, the good of the earth, or the good of all creation (or the good of God.)**

Spiritual disciplines can include body, mind, heart, or spirit activity. We believe that spiritual disciplines affect our entire well-being—our whole selves.

Let me give you some examples of my own spiritual disciplines to give you an idea of the range of possibilities:

- Some activities are ongoing and are integrated into my regular schedule: doing InterPlay as often as possible, going to the gym to do stretches for my lower back and to swim, writing regularly, and being at church on Sunday morning when I am in town.

- Some activities are more focused on something I have chosen to work on. For example, because I am an introvert, I have been practicing extrovert skills in social situations. (Being extroverted in my work is not usually a problem.) I practice initiating and carrying on social conversations, sharing my own stories and information, and assuming that others are interested. I practice "taking up space" in groups and being relaxed when the attention is on me. When I am in public I try to lighten my expression with at least a half-smile.

> • • • • • • • • •
> **I practice realizing that I really don't know how long I will live, and that I shouldn't put off doing what is most important to me until later in life.**

- Some activities are more internal. When I see young people on the street, I imagine them to be honor students in their schools, regardless of their attitude, dress, or racial or ethnic background. When I think of people in other parts of the world, I think of them as brothers and sisters, regardless of the relationship between my country's government and theirs. Every once in a while I include in my consciousness as much of the universe as I can imagine.

- I practice looking for the good in myself, others, and in the world, and practice suspending judgment and criticism. I practice affirming others. I look for the gifts in children and young people.

- I practice realizing that I really don't know how long I will live, and that I shouldn't put off doing what is most important to me until later in life.

- I recycle, I brush my teeth twice a day, I try to call my parents with some regularity, I bring to mind people that I care about, I pay attention to my house plants, I take deep breaths often, I donate money, I laugh a lot.

- There are also spiritual disciplines that I work on but with varying degrees of success: flossing, imagining that those who hold opposing political views from mine are actually well intentioned, writing to my friends, doing my own artwork, making the bed, paying attention to my posture and alignment, not letting the piles of paperwork in my office get too high or too numerous.

You can reframe your "pictures" of spiritual disciplines: you can change your experience and behavior with practice; you don't need to focus directly on a supreme being in order to call your work or play "spiritual"; spiritual disciplines need not be profound—they can be simple and direct; **all spiritual disciplines are physical and are about being in your body, not escaping it.**

At the beginning of each InterPlay class, which we teach to help people reclaim their physicality, we warm up. One of the exercises is to stand with your feet spread widely apart and then make big slow circles with your hips. When we name this a spiritual discipline, people invariably laugh. Moving one's hips seems almost completely opposite to how people picture spiritual disciplines. We include these exercises each time because we believe that we will be better off individually and culturally if we practice them regularly.

**We believe that the most direct way to change your life is to change your physical activity.** Change involves practicing something new. Many of our models of therapy are based on the idea that if I change my mind my life will change: if I figure out what the "problem" is, or gain insight into my behavior, then it will fix itself. But it isn't enough to just "decide." There must be some repetition of a new or different activity. That could include changing the way you think, which is, of course, physical activity.

Here is some more body wisdom about spiritual disciplines:

- **Practicing a spiritual discipline may actually teach me that I am not going to change all that much**, or that the change isn't going to match my pictures. Going to the gym may not give me a perfectly toned body. Practicing being an extrovert may not change my introversion. Looking at people of other races or social classes differently may not eliminate my prejudices. Perhaps rather than changing me, these disciplines will only provide some balance or moderation.

- **You can see spiritual disciplines as play rather than work, as choice rather than obligation.** There are huge pressures in secular culture to "fix" ourselves—to be better people. We should be thinner, prettier, richer, sexier, or smarter. In religious culture, spiritual disciplines are often motivated by a sense of obligation. They are requirements or duties, sometimes even punishments—certainly not fun. Take your spiritual disciplines lightly!

- **We do not have to be better.** Actually, one of the spiritual disciplines that we might practice is to accept ourselves just as we are. We are not obligated to change. We can, though, choose to practice something new. We can approach a new spiritual discipline with a sense of amusement and ease rather than a sense of drudgery. If it doesn't work out the way we might have hoped, then we can also let it go.

- **Spiritual disciplines should lead to the good for ourselves, others, the earth, or all of creation (God).** To claim what is good for *me* may be difficult. We may have learned that to do something for our own good is self-indulgent and, therefore, wrong. We may have learned that we must deny ourselves good in order for others to have good. Our pictures about sacrifice and giving may make it difficult for us to "have."

Here is the truth: **claiming goodness for ourselves can make it easier to give to others.** There is a split in our culture between giving and receiving. They are seen as mutually exclusive. What if we were to practice having both at once? They can actually happen at the same time. Even though it may be difficult for us to conceptualize this, our bodies can handle it quite easily. Try this simple exercise: find a friend and give him or her a shoulder rub. Pay attention to receiving from this activity in the same moment that you are giving to them. How does that feel? Is it possible to both give and receive in the same moment?

- **Despite our pictures that spiritual disciplines are solitary affairs, they can often be practiced more effectively in community.** It may help to have a jogging partner, for example, or to get the whole family to conserve water or recycle. It may help to tell someone else what you are practicing to get support or have accountability. If you have a particularly helpful discipline, perhaps others would like to practice it too. Some spiritual disciplines only make sense in community: singing in a choir, sharing a meal, working for political change, building a house for Habitat for Humanity, attending public worship or rituals or ceremonies.

- **It may be difficult for us to tell the difference between something that is really good for us and something that may seem good in the moment but has negative consequences or aftereffects.** We may seek satisfaction in transitory or unhealthy ways through over–eating, smoking, drinking, gambling, fighting, unsafe sex, or taking physical risks.

**To redefine spiritual disciplines is to open up a whole**

**new territory to play in, a place of fullness and abundance.** It is not a separate place that we only visit from time to time. Instead, it can surround every moment of our lives. The first step is to notice what you desire for yourself, others, or the world. What concrete steps can you take toward having this? Work incrementally. Don't bite off more than you can chew to begin with. Remember to keep your sense of humor. Get someone else involved in the process—sharing your intention with others may help you accomplish it. As time goes on, reevaluate your spiritual disciplines. Feel free to let go of them or shift them to something else. Notice any changes in your bodyspirit that occur from practicing spiritual disciplines and celebrate these changes.

**RESULTS** *You can have spiritual disciplines of all different sorts. They can create a structure for getting what you want out of life, for having goodness that you may be missing, or for creating grace for others in the world.*

• • • • • • • • • • • • • • • • • • • • • •

*We often think that our practices and spiritual disciplines are solitary affairs, things we do on our own. I believe, based on much of my experience, that it is more effective to have the support of community. We need to practice together.*

*I was preaching in a church in Minnesota, and I was talking about this powerful aspect of community. I confessed that I was having trouble with one of my spiritual disciplines—flossing. Despite numerous dental hygienist harangues, I still wasn't flossing regularly.*

*I told the congregation that I was convinced that I was experiencing this difficulty because I wasn't flossing in community. (This may have been the first time in the world that the subject of flossing came up in a sermon.) When the offering was taken up and brought forward, someone had placed a small container of dental floss in the offering plate. It was a sign.*

*Now I no longer floss alone. Every time I pull out my container of thin white string (cinnamon flavored), I think of all those folks in Minnesota. My flossing record is steadily improving!*

# Exformation: The Antidote for the Information Age

**ADVICE** *We are bombarded by information. It is enter-ing our bodies and lives in great quantities. If you want bal-ance in your life, find ways to move some of that information out of your body. We call this process "exformation."*

All information is physical. Our bodies take it in, "have it," process it. It enters our bodies in a variety of ways: the five senses we memorized as children—seeing, hearing, touching, tasting, and smelling—as well as others that are harder to describe or articulate, like our kinesthetic response to our own and others' movement.

Much of the information we receive is concrete and straightforward: I see smoke in the distance, I hear a bus go by, I feel the warmth of the sun, I read a paragraph in a magazine. Other times the information may be more subtle: I enter a room and something seems different, I meet a friend on the street and they don't quite seem themselves, I suddenly remember an incident from a long time ago but I don't really know why it came to mind, I have a strange dream.

**No matter how important or unimportant each bit of information may be, if it reaches my body, it is in me.** It becomes part of my bodyspirit. It is physical. I may pass by a newsstand and catch a glimpse of a disturbing headline. That headline is now part of my physical experi-ence whether I want it there or not.

Our culture drowns us in information. Advertisements are everywhere; phones, faxes, and now modems stream messages into our lives; there are newspapers, magazines, and books galore to read; we travel to many different places full of old and new data. Even the cereal box that sits in front of us at the breakfast table screams for our attention.

**Information accumulates in our bodies: piling up, clogging our systems, getting stuck.** This can be dangerous.

So what do we do?

**We exform.**

**If information is the movement of data into our bodies, then exformation is the reverse. It is a word we invented to describe the movement of data outward.**

• • • • • • • • •
**Exformational activities may differ from person to person. You may need a quiet activity while I may need one that is highly physical.**

Exformation may involve actually moving "stuff" out of our bodies in some sort of physical expression, or it may just mean that the data moves from deep inside to closer to the surface. For example, through exformation, I may become aware that I was deeply disturbed by a recent event reported in the news. Or I may use exformation to give that concern direct physical expression, to try to shift or relieve my disturbance.

You may believe that you can put aside internal data just by deciding to. "I'm not going to think about that," or "I'm not going to let that affect me." But if information is physical, it may take direct physical activity to process, integrate, express, react, or unload.

**Many activities are "exformational"**: the arts, spiritual practices, sports and exercise, hobbies or crafts, conversation and "processing," journaling, gardening, playing, making love, therapy, body work. Any of these activities can give our bodyspirits room to breathe, as well as actually moving out the stuff that is collecting in us.

Can you identify the activities in your own life that are exformational? What helps you move "stuff" out of your body? Do you have enough exformational activity in your life to balance the amount of information that is coming in?

Here are some characteristics of exformational activities:

- **Exformational activities often involve some repetitive action.** If you are physically engaged in a task that doesn't require your complete attention, your inner information can float to the surface in an unplanned way. Many hobby and craft activities are repetitive: carving, knitting, needlework, weaving. Walking, running, swimming, and cross–country skiing may also have the same effect. Many traditional spiritual practices involve physical repetition. Even housework, like sweeping or washing the dishes, may be exformational.

- **Exformational activities often increase breathing and circulation:** sports, exercise, active play, making love, and singing, for example. Taking a deep breath may be the simplest and most accessible exformational activity. Many traditional spiritual disciplines focus on breathing. Sighing and shaking all or parts of the body are also easy to do and highly effective.

- **Exformational activities often involve the act of creating something or making something happen.** When we create, we bring our own information to bear on the creation. We are making decisions based on our own sense of shape, taste, desire, and design. You could be creating a painting or a pie, shaping a pot or arranging the furniture in your home, growing a garden or making up a song. To enjoy the exformational effects of creativity, we may need to "explode" some of our pictures about who is creative and what is "art." If we are not great artists, we may have trouble claiming our own creativity or even getting involved in creative forms.

- **Both the process and the result of exformation are often nonverbal.** Dancing or moving, painting or sighing are all nonverbal. The information they elicit may also be difficult to put into words. Even so, we can still "have" the grace of the exformation.

- **Exformation is sometimes indirect.** I may not even know what needs to be exformed. If I get involved in an activity that I know is exformational for me, the inner information will often present itself.

- **Exformational activities may differ from person to person.** You may need a quiet activity while I may need one that is highly physical. We need to pay attention to our own experience to determine what works for each of us. We may stumble across an exformational form by accident.

- **Some activities border on exformation but can go either way.** A conversation can be exformational unless the other person is doing all the talking. Reading a book or listening to a speaker can be exformational if our own information is being elicited.

- **When we exform, we may actually be releasing other people's information.** We take in "stuff" at a body-to-body level from others. It may be difficult for us to tell what is our own and what is not. If I am around someone who is depressed, for example, then I may begin to feel depressed. Exformation can help us release that information.

- You may think that exformation needs to be deeply cathartic—emotionally releasing but also taxing, a "big deal." Actually, though, **"fun" is a good sign of exformation.** What activities do you particularly enjoy or delight in? What makes you laugh? Laughter is excellent exformation.

If you pay attention to your own experience, it will be easy for you to identify exformation in your life. You will begin to notice what you do that helps you balance the information glut in your life. Once you identify these activities, you can have more of them. You will feel much better, and others will enjoy being around you more!

Exformation and the physicality of grace are closely related. Exformation creates grace. Notice what creates grace for you: these are your exformational activities.

Exformation is central to the practice of InterPlay. (There is more information about InterPlay beginning on page 109.) The InterPlay technique has most of the characteristics that I have just described:

- **It is physically active**, so it increases breathing and circulation.

- **It allows each of us to use our own physical vocabulary**, which creates room for our own individual content.

- **It includes many different forms,** so individuals are likely to find one that is particularly exformational for them.

- **There are many opportunities for nonverbal expression**, and an honoring of the information or experience that is elicited even if it is difficult to articulate.

- **There is lots of room for creativity**, and participants are encouraged to claim their huge creative possibilities.

- **It encourages fun.**

**Exformation can heal splits.** It moves "stuff" out of the way. It clears our bodyspirits so we can be fully ourselves. To find a balance between information and exformation in our lives is a crucial task.

**RESULTS** *Exformation provides an excellent way to move excess "stuff" out of your body. It will increase your sense of openness and your ability to handle the overwhelming amount of information coming into your life.*

● ● ● ● ● ● ● ● ● ● ● ● ● ● ● ● ● ● ● ● ● ●

*I experience the "deals" in my life over long periods of time. The oscillation of my emotional life consists of relatively flat, gentle curves, at least compared to the seismographic drama of many of my friends. If you were to ask me on any particular day how I was doing, I would likely answer, "Fine." It would be a true answer, not just a polite one. I would also be quite able to identify the longer–term questions or struggles, though. (Just want to prove that I am not in denial!)*

*I still need to exform, however. Even though I may not experience the need urgently, and I may use it as much for research as release, it still feels good for my bodyspirit to move some "stuff" around or out.*

*In InterPlay, one of my favorite exformational forms is a very simple one. Either sitting or lying down, I let one hand move freely around. I try to let my hand lead rather than controlling it or thinking ahead about where it is going. It helps to have music in the background. I should probably be able to practice this on my own at home, but it usually happens in one of our classes or workshops.*

*Often I don't know what it is that wants to come out. But "it" usually does, and it is almost always fascinating, if I do say so myself.*

*Before we invented the idea of "exformation," I discovered a similar experience dying fabric for my artwork. The dye pot needs to be constantly stirred anywhere from fifteen minutes to an hour. I would sit on the edge of the tub in my bathroom with the fabric in a five–gallon pickle barrel from McDonald's. As I gently stirred, I would notice changes in my body. My thoughts would drift and*

*wander in the most wonderful ways. I would be both relaxed and
energized.*

*As I paid more attention, I noticed that this also happened in
other settings: when the water was running down my body in
the shower, as I drifted away during a concert or lecture or sermon, as I washed the dishes unhurriedly. Now I savor those
moments (especially the ones in the shower!)*

# Giving and Getting More Affirmation

 **ADVICE**  *You will be happier if you give and receive more affirmation in your life.*

**Early in our lives someone started telling us what we were doing wrong:** don't touch that, don't go there, don't do that. As we got older, more mobile, and more autonomous, we received more and more messages about what we shouldn't be doing. Don't slouch, don't talk with your mouth full, don't put your elbows on the table, don't yell, don't get out of your seat, don't speak unless spoken to, don't swear, don't wear those clothes, don't hang around those people.

Although we may have also been praised, negative behavior usually gets more attention, and there is more energy behind the communication. There is less need for comment if a child is playing quietly in the middle of the living room floor than if she is pounding on the cat or sticking a pair of scissors in a light socket.

Most of our institutions—families, schools, churches, organizations, the workplace—demand a high level of fitting in. Institutions rely heavily on critique to make that happen. Conformity and compliance are encouraged, if not enforced.

It is appropriate to learn how to behave in public, to know how to fit in with others, and understand the balance between individual and community needs. But what is the cost of living in a culture of critique?

**We lose our sense of choice, of individuality, of expressiveness and abandon, of ecstasy, creativity, discovery. We may be unable to tell when we need to behave and when we can let go. If we are criticized too severely, we may lose our sense of self–confidence and self–esteem.**

Affirmation needs to be practiced as much as possible to balance the amount of criticism in our lives.

To have affirmation is to shift the way you look at

● ● ● ● ● ● ● ● ●
**Affirmation is good for the body. It makes us open, energized, relaxed, and responsive. It increases self-esteem and decreases our insecurity.**

life, at others, and at yourself. You look at what is right rather than what is wrong. You focus on what is to be celebrated rather than what needs to be fixed.

We believe that affirmation can create just as much growth and change as criticism can.

Criticism is hard on the body. It makes us tight, closed, reluctant, and resistant. Just imagine someone calling you a stupid fool. How does that feel in your body?

Affirmation, on the other hand, is good for the body. It makes us open, energized, relaxed, and responsive. It increases self–esteem and decreases our insecurity. It encourages truthfulness rather than denial. Imagine someone telling you that you are smart or beautiful. How does that feel?

When we focus on critique, we rob our bodies of pleasure. If I focus on what I didn't like about a performance I have just seen, for example, I may drown out any of the positive experiences I had. I will be left with the negative in my body.

Are you a critic or an affirmer? During the drive home after a party, do you praise the other guests or gossip about them? When you have just completed some job or project, do you celebrate the accomplishment or catalog its short-comings? When someone praises you, do you bask in it or brush it aside?

Much of our self–image is based on how others respond to who we are and what we do. **We are hungry for these messages, especially the positive ones.** We need to be told what we are doing right, what others appreciate in us, what gifts they see. "You are so patient with your chil-dren," "I really appreciated the support you gave me when my mother was sick," "You are really great at organizing things," "I love your cooking!"

Personally, I can never get enough affirmation. Therefore, I assume that I can never give too much to others. To prac-tice affirmation is to give and receive grace. To learn to affirm others is a great first step to take toward affirming ourselves. **If I look for the best in others, I may learn to be more forgiving of myself and to celebrate who I am and what I do.**

Sometimes we are our own worst critics, obsessing about our shortcomings and mistakes, feeling guilty about what we have done or not done. We dwell on every small nega-tive detail. We focus on our imperfections.

It may be a good thing to be able to admit what we have done wrong, or see where we might improve, but I think we are overpracticed at this. We have been taught to be modest and humble, to deflect praise, and to avoid claim-ing credit—"tooting our own horn." But what does this do to our sense of self? What does it do to our self–confidence to be encouraged to accept blame but discouraged from asking for or receiving affirmation, reassurance, or praise?

**Affirmation is a practice, a spiritual discipline.** It is simple to do but may be unfamiliar. If we are primarily used to criticizing or being criticized, it may seem like a daunting pattern to reverse. But by taking the simple steps of finding ways to affirm ourselves and others, it will become easier to both do and "have."

Begin by noticing those around you. What do you like about someone else—who they are or what they do? Be more aware of that and enjoy it. "Have" the grace of that appreciation in your own body. If it is possible, tell the person as well. You will both benefit. **Practice focusing on the positive aspects of the information that surrounds you. What do you see, hear, taste, touch, smell, sense, remember, or imagine that increases your sense of enjoyment or well-being?** Pay attention to that. When you see a performance, for example, practice noting to yourself or others what you really liked or enjoyed. Don't even bother to articulate what you disliked. When you think about someone, look for the good, notice it to yourself, and say it aloud.

> • • • • • • • • •
> What would happen if we assumed that it was not our job to judge, or "fix" other people, situations, creations, or even ourselves. Would the world fall apart?

We know about the power of positive reinforcement. Often, though, we pair it directly with criticism. We use a few positive remarks about someone or a situation to lead up to a critique: "I like this and this and this about you, but...." Don't we know that it is the part that comes after that big "but" that is really the truth? The affirmation that came before is completely negated. As a practice, it is possible to say only the first part of the statement, even if in the beginning the critical conclusion still rings in our heads.

What would happen if we assumed that it was not our job to judge or "fix" other people, situations, creations, or even ourselves? Would the world fall apart? This may be a radical idea. Imagine yourself as a manager in a business. Could you operate primarily through a process of affirmation? And could you do that as an activity of grace-making rather than seeing it as a subtle way to manipulate others? Can you imagine the members of one party in

Congress affirming the members of the other party? Can you imagine only giving positive messages to your spouse or partner? If this sounds difficult or unlikely, it is an indication of the power of the culture of critique.

I am not suggesting that we eliminate all criticism but that we find a balance between affirmation and critique. **It is not necessary to be ruled by a culture of criticism. The repeated practice of small acts of affirmation can change our own lives and the lives of others.**

To decrease the amount of judgment in our lives is transforming and liberating. To be easier on ourselves and others can radically increase the amount of enjoyment we get from life. We carry within us a stream of negative critical voices, which we in turn communicate in direct and subtle ways to others. Giving and receiving affirmation is the simplest and most direct way to reduce the effect of the critical voice in ourselves and in our culture.

**RESULTS**   *Affirmation is one of the simplest but most rewarding spiritual disciplines to practice. It is a great joy to our bodyspirits to both give and receive it.*

• • • • • • • • • • • • • • • • • • • • • •

*I truly believe that I deserve attention and affirmation for the good things I do, even if they are routine and expected. Take housework, for example. I know it is my duty to make my bed, keep the dirty dishes from overwhelming me, and to occasionally dust and vacuum. Millions of people across the country and around the world perform these tasks all the time with little fanfare. I will fulfill my housework obligation, but I want the fanfare, too.*

*I have found, though, that it is pretty easy to get the applause that I want. First, I look for someone to whom I can point out my* good deeds. It doesn't work to wait until someone notices what I have done. I seek out recognition and ask for it! Hopefully the person I choose will respond in a positive and appreciative manner.

Sometimes this doesn't work. The other person may not be getting the applause they deserve, making them stingy about giving it to me. In this case, I immediately move into the applause–giving role. Hopefully this will change his or her sour disposition.

But even if there is no one around, I can congratulate myself. Actually or imaginatively, I throw my hands in the air like a gymnast after a perfect routine and shout out a big fat "yes!"

# How to Be a
# Body Intellectual

**ADVICE**  *Use the information that is literally at your fingertips—the wisdom that comes from noticing and articulating your personal experience.*

Cynthia and I teach people to be "body intellectuals." When we describe ourselves as body intellectuals to audiences, they often laugh. This is an unexpected combination of terms.

The laughter this phrase evokes reveals the split in our culture between body and mind. Smart football players? Body–building philosophers? Articulate dancers? The "picture" is that you can have one or the other but not both. We want to heal that split.

To be a body intellectual is not to get stuck in the analytical. Nor is it about ignoring heart or spirit. It is really just practicing "being smart" about your body and the fullness it includes. As you practice noticing your experience you will get better at it, and you will also find more ways to articulate it.

Do you want to be a body intellectual? Here's how to become one:

- Pay attention to the fullness of your physical experience.

- Practice putting words around your experience.

- Leap over categories and claim interrelationships.

- Look for wholeness rather than separation.

- Claim individual authority as well as the wisdom of the community.

- "Think" with your whole body.

- Seek to identify splits and heal them.

- Avoid language that encourages split thinking.

- Trace the experiential roots of your beliefs.

- Identify the differences between knowledge that comes from personal experience and that which has been drilled into you by others.

- Evaluate others' information in relation to your own experience.

- Honor differences in personal experience.

The marvelous part of "having it all" is that the physical and the intellectual are not split. Isn't my head part of my body? Isn't thinking physical activity? To be articulate about our physical experience is a marvelous ability to have. To include the wholeness of our physicality changes the way we "think," and as we change the way we think, we open up new possibilities for living our lives more fully.

**RESULTS**   *To heal the splits between mind, body, heart, and spirit means that our wisdom can be drawn from all those areas, rather than just one. It will make our "knowing" richer and deeper.*

• • • • • • • • • • • • • • • • • • • • •

*Have you ever seen those large plastic disk–shaped collars that the vet puts on a dog to keep it from scratching its head? Perhaps on a particular day of the year, everyone (humans, that is) should have to wear one of those as a symbol of the way we treat the relationship between our heads and bodies.*

*We speak and behave as if there is some great barrier or divide that occurs right at the neck. A friend of mine used to say that we treat our bodies like biological Toyotas. They transport our brains from one spot to another and then get parked for long periods of time.*

*We are taught at an early age to sit still, which is a valuable but overpracticed skill for most of us. We learn that this is the proper mode for learning and for praying. Keep your body still if you want your mind to work, we are told.*

*On the other hand, when we pay attention to our bodies we tend to ignore our heads. If someone asked us to check in with our bodies we would probably search around for any aches and pains (from the neck down), look for signs of emotional or digestive activity (closely related), or assess the general state of our energy.*

*I doubt, however, that most of us would report back about what we were seeing or hearing, and certainly not what we were thinking. But isn't this all physical experience? Body stuff?*

*We will certainly experience splits between the mind stuff and all the other stuff until we can take off our giant neck collars.*

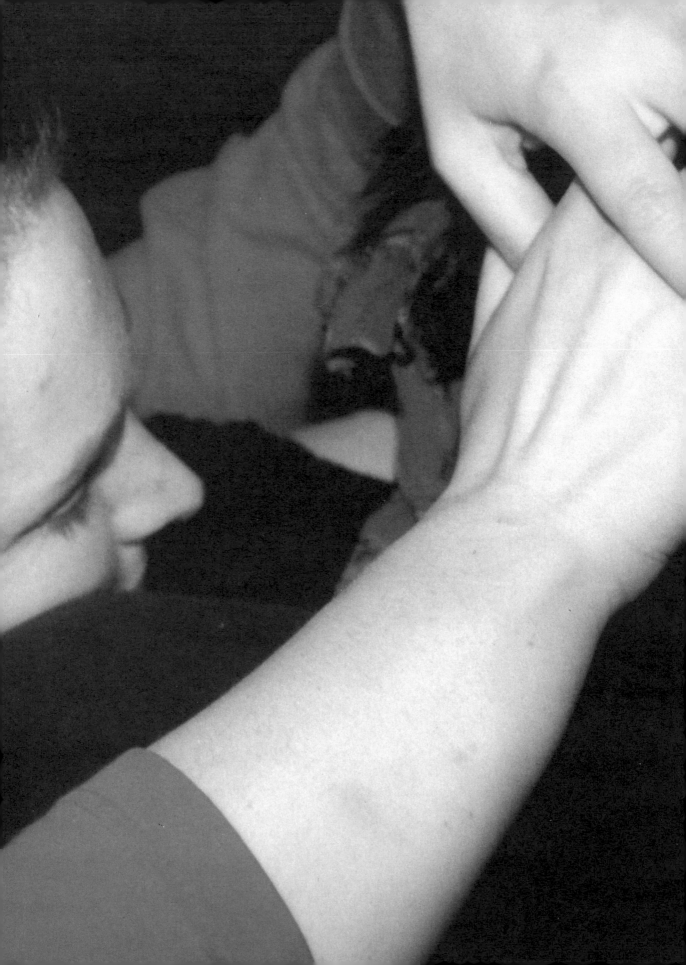

# Dancing into the Age of Reintegration

Any system of ideas, beliefs, or practices is ultimately rooted in the direct experience of those who develop the system, even if it has "universal" intentions. The ideas presented here come out of the experience of two people with uncommon vocations: **we are performers, primarily trained as dancers, and we are church leaders in mainline Protestant denominations.** A strange combination? Yes, it is. There aren't many of us in the country.

But it has put us in the perfect position to bridge the gap between body and spirit, one of the primary splits in our culture that needs healing. The dance community is embodied but distrusts spirit. The church has spirit–knowing but fears the body. To knit the two communities together, we have had to develop whole new ways of thinking, working, playing, and being.

Cynthia and I have worked together as teachers, performers, writers, theologians, choreographers, and speakers since 1979.

For many years we co–directed Body & Soul Dance Company with our colleague, Judith Rock. We described ourselves as a modern dance company with a special interest in theological themes and images. **We found ourselves perched between the dance world and the world of the church.** All three of us worked actively in both spheres. **These were communities which only rarely intersected and generally regarded each other**

**with some suspicion.** We used to joke that, reflecting our name, our mission was to convince church people that they had bodies and the dance community that it could have a soul.

The modern dance world at the time was obsessed with abstraction. Bodies were shapes and movement in space. The modern dance "face" was emblematic: neutral and unexpressive. In contrast, we wanted to choreograph dances about people and relationships. Our work dealt with our humanity—the universal issues embedded in our everyday lives. It was the spark of identity or spirit that we felt was missing from most modern dance at the time.

● ● ● ● ● ● ● ● ●

**It was so much easier to do an improvised piece than to try to dance our choreography while dodging baptismal fonts, floral arrangements, and communion tables.**

We traveled around the country doing performances and workshops, often in churches, often for people with relatively little experience with dance. In our workshops, we needed to include many levels of ability. **We knew that many would be threatened by the idea of dancing, that many are uncomfortable in their bodies.**

**We discovered the tool of improvisation.** It allowed everyone to work at their own level. Individuals and groups found their own way of moving. It let the unexpected emerge. People learned about themselves. We also used improvisation in performance, especially in eccentrically–arranged church spaces. It was so much easier to do an improvised piece than to try to dance our choreography while dodging baptismal fonts, floral arrangements, and communion tables.

Our audiences were often made up of people who were unfamiliar with modern dance. Some may have seen it on public television. Some may have caught a performance by one of the major touring companies. But this was not the crowd who would normally troop off to a downtown loft to see experimental dance.

I'm sure it seemed unlikely to many that we were working in the church. Although some dancers have been doing sacred or liturgical dance for years, many religious traditions have or have had prohibitions against dancing. And in any religious space, there are always serious questions about appropriateness (even whether dancers should have bare feet or not).

**Perched as we were between these two estranged worlds, we built bridges. We talked. We articulated. We theologized. We wove the words around the dancing. We talked about bodies to church people. We included spirit in our work in the dance world.**

This history shaped our current work. **We are still bridging worlds that need integration.** We are still discovering non–threatening ways to let all sorts of different people be in their bodies. We are still talking—theologizing and philosophizing—about what we know.

After Body & Soul Dance Company ended in 1988, Cynthia and I formed a new dance company devoted to improvisation. We named it WING IT! Performance Ensemble. We also began to systematize our methods for teaching our style of improvisation, which we called InterPlay. As our teaching and performing developed, it quickly became apparent that our work had applications beyond the church.

Our early Body & Soul process of straddling the worlds of dance and the church had encouraged us, even demanded that we create connections that were missing in many parts of contemporary life—**connections that allowed people to have a sense of wholeness, to bring all the parts of themselves together.** From the beginning we were bridging the body/spirit split, a split that demanded that in certain times and places we shut off parts of ourselves in order to function, to be accepted, or just to match others' expectations.

It became clear that what we had to say was not just for dancers or for those interested in moving or performing, but for anyone who had a body. Our audience was not just church people, but **anyone who sought a sense of wholeness, fullness, and integrity that may have been missing in their lives**, whether or not they are part of a theological or spiritual tradition.

Gradually, a new practice and philosophy, which we called InterPlay, evolved. InterPlay wove together physical activities that almost any willing body could do, with a set of new ideas about the wholeness of our experience.

Although InterPlay is firmly based in activity and exploration, the ideas that are integral to this work can be applied to one's life regardless of how willing one is to "play." This is why we describe InterPlay both as a practice and a philosophy.

# InterPlay Is a Great Way to Have It All

**InterPlay is the system Cynthia and I have been creating since 1989.** We wanted a clear framework in which to explore body/spirit/mind/heart connections, we wanted the language to explain our ideas, and we wanted ways to live the principles we espoused.

**InterPlay is a philosophy and technique—a way of thinking and a way of doing.** It is a set of ideas as well as a physical technique—a way of playing—that we teach to groups of people. It is constantly changing.

InterPlay is the ongoing laboratory for our research. The ideas presented in this book have come out of years of teaching, performing, writing, debating, and playing with lots of different folk all over the country and the world.

InterPlay is easier to experience than describe, but here are some of the its characteristics:

- **It is a practice that any body can do.** It requires no previous experience or training and respects the limitations and celebrates the possibilities of each body. Willingness is probably the most important quality to have.

- **It allows room for individual information.** We each bring different gifts; we each have different experience.

- **It values and creates community.** We are not only individual bodies, but we are connected at a deeply physical level as well. We gain support, information, and energy from others.

- **It allows us to bring all parts of ourselves together:** body, mind, heart, spirit. It breaks through the artificiality of those categories.

- **It is devoted to fun.** We choose a context of play rather than work. We choose joy rather than struggle.

We believe that to change, you have to change more than your mind, you have to change what you do. **Change takes practice.** We believe that the fullness in our lives is from having both the philosophy and the practice of InterPlay. But there are lots of different ways to change. InterPlay can affect your life no matter how much of your body you are willing to get involved.

> • • • • • • • • •
> We dare to stand in front of others without a script or choreography or a score and expect something to emerge, as scary as that might seem to some people.

**InterPlay is rooted in artistic forms:** dance, theater, vocal music. But more fundamentally, it is rooted in the creative possibilities of the body. **What are all the things a body can do, either alone or with other bodies?**

To claim our ability to create or perform in our culture is difficult. Through the media and live performance we are exposed to the best in the performance arts—the best in the entire nation and even the world. How could we possibly compare ourselves to that? How many of us claim to be a dancer, or actor, or singer? As Cynthia and I describe our work to others, we are sometimes reluctant to use the word "dance." We know that it will block some people from even walking through the door because they are certain they can't "dance."

**InterPlay is improvisational.** We make up stuff in the moment without rehearsal both individually and in groups. We dare to stand in front of others without a script or choreography or a score and expect something to emerge, as scary as that might seem to some people.

In InterPlay we reclaim our ability not only to make up "stuff" using the resources of our body and experience, but to share it with others as well. InterPlay participants create and perform, and they do it on the spot. We have done this with people of all ages and all abilities. It is marvelously possible, and the material that is created is powerful, touching, poignant, hilarious, revelatory, exuberant, joyful.

**If we can step through our reticence, our fear of embarrassment, our insecurity, or our desire for invisibility, the results can be incredible. The stories and dances and songs that people create are amazing.**

To accomplish this we move in gentle steps, incremental ones, rooting the experience firmly in play, having fun, being easy and relaxed, and affirmation. "Yes!" we say as often as we can to each other and ourselves.

We concentrate on forms in which creativity is easily released. It is the underlying structure that provides our security and makes it possible for us to play together in wonderfully complex ways.

Every body is different and each has its own way of being, moving, and creating. InterPlay provides plenty of opportunities for that individuality. **We don't prescribe a particular way of doing things, but instead give people the room to do the things that they do best or most easily.** Most of our forms are also relational, so there is a lot of sharing of information, trying on what someone else does, creating something new in between what you and I do.

Let me give you an example of one of our "forms." What happens if we play with following and leading? First I will follow what you do for a time, and then you will follow me. We will use both movement and sound. Then we will play around with the following and leading agreement so that it moves back and forth in the moment. Within this structure there is plenty of opportunity for me to do what

I do best, for you to do the same, and for us to find new possibilities together.

Then within this following and leading structure we will try other experiments. We will play with using more and less space between our bodies, with repetition, with fullness of movement, with stillness, with moving in and out of eye contact with each other. These possibilities are the "tools" we use to create pieces that are interesting to do and to watch.

To learn about these tools is a little like adding new tango steps in ballroom dancing. Each one gives us new possibilities for dancing a wonderful tango together. The difference is that in InterPlay the tools have to do with form rather than content. Rather than learning specific new steps (or words or sounds) we are learning more about how to shape the steps (or words or sounds) that come up in the moment. These, of course, are different every time.

**Incremental steps and clear simple structures are two of the primary characteristics of InterPlay.** We choose to focus on simple tasks rather than inner information. We don't ask people to "dance their feelings" for example. Instead we will say to a whole group, "Let's play with walking, stopping, and running, everyone deciding on their own when to do each one." Afterwards, we will take some time to notice what comes up for us when we do this. The inner information surfaces by choice rather than on demand.

**The ability to make choices about what we do or how we respond also insures that any body can participate, no matter what shape it is in.** InterPlay makes room for all ages and abilities. It lets us work around our stiff or sore parts—or our fear—and it allows for the changes our bodies go through as they age. If my partner jumps higher than I can, I adjust the movement to fit my body. If we have been playing exuberantly and run out of breath, we can find slower or quieter ways to play. The important point is that we are still part of the creative conversation. We don't need to absent ourselves because we can't move like another.

**Within any set of limitations there is the possibility for fullness.** If you can only move one arm, move it fully! If you can only sing one note, sing it loudly! If you only have one story to tell, tell it with gusto! Each of us is ripe with creative possibilities. Each has a special part to play in the whole piece.

**We reclaim the play of childhood, but add to it all the information, skill, complexity, and subtlety that we have acquired as adults.** It is amazing what we can create in the moment if we bring all this information to bear. Our performance company creates entire evenings of improvised work, and we have approached all sorts of subjects. Our concerts have had titles like "God, Sex and Power," "Life and Death," "Lies and Dreams." Participants in our classes and workshops have also created many different pieces that have power and integrity, all based on a few basic forms and some common agreements, but no rehearsal.

We work with movement, story, and songs. Within each of these forms are many variations and combinations: solos, duets, small and large group pieces, songs to accompany dances, stories that include movement and sound. The list goes on and on. Because there are so many forms to choose from, almost everyone will find one that is particularly effective for them, one they particularly enjoy. We encourage participants to notice which forms are most rewarding for them and which are most challenging. Although there is growth that can come from exploring new territory, we also value savoring the experience that comes from working in our comfort zones. We are pushed to grow in our culture. We need more time to just be who we are rather than always striving toward what we might become.

**The nature of our work creates community.** There is

no quicker way to build relationship between people than to move, sing, or tell stories together. As Plato said: "You can learn more about another in an hour of play than in a lifetime of conversation." For two people to play together creates instant connection. The bodyspirit is immediately revealed. We may have trouble remembering our partner's name, but we already know a great deal about them, and they know about us as well. We find that the participants in our classes and workshops are hungry for that kind of connection, one that goes deeper than small talk.

**Even the work that we do as individuals is rooted in community. We rely on the support and affirmation of those around us—to witness us and to receive our gifts.**

InterPlay not only espouses the possibility and necessity of reintegrating body, mind, heart, and spirit, but allows us to practice it as well. To play together in this way naturally elicits all of our information. Our bodies are active, our thoughts are engaged, we are allowed to feel, and to experience connection and mystery all at once. The effects are almost immediate. We breathe more fully and more easily, we are stimulated by our own inner information and ideas, our awareness of others is increased, and we feel lighter and less encumbered.

**"Fun" is treated with such ambivalence in our culture.** We know that having fun is a good experience for our bodies—it is pleasurable. We are constantly being enjoined by advertising to buy things that will increase our "fun quotient." Even bizarre things like gum or cigarettes are supposed to be "fun." At the same time, however, we trivialize fun. If something is fun, it can't be very important, or profound, or productive. It might even be embarrassing or silly, for goodness' sake.

"Fun" may be difficult to define, but we can reclaim the fullness of the experience. When we ask people to brainstorm words that come to mind in relationship to the word "fun," we begin to recognize the power of the experience: delight, laughter, mystery, unselfconscious, free, play, satisfying, enlivening, connected, easy going, light–hearted, smile, brightness, tingly. **Why wouldn't we want more of this in our lives?**

There are many ways to heal splits, but to get one's entire being into the act—**to bring all of our intellectual, emotional, physical, and spiritual gifts together in one place** is, from our experience, the most effective and the most fun.

**We have learned that we don't need to focus on pain in order to grow. We can choose instead to look for the good, to build on our strengths, to celebrate what we can do rather than struggle with what we can't.** We know that thinking without breathing is impossible, that the concrete and the mysterious always exist in the same moment, that fear of embarrassment can rob us of joy, that truth will emerge if we get out of its way, that what we can "see" of our gifts is only the "tip of the iceberg," that there are brains in our entire bodies, and that we can approach our lives with a sense of knowing rather than not knowing.

**Doing InterPlay has taught us all of these things.**

# InterPlay & Lessons about Life

**The lessons of InterPlay are life lessons.** Since each person works so directly with her or his own information, there is always a close relationship between what we come up with when we play and all the rest of our lives. InterPlay teaches us about ourselves, each other and the world.

Here is some of what it has to offer.

**InterPlay teaches us that every bodyspirit is different.** Looking at any crowd of people, this is self–evident. But let's take the next step: if every bodyspirit is different, we may have very different experiences. If we have different experience, we are likely to have different opinions and beliefs. We may even have a completely different sense of what is true.

Early on in our classes we play with following and leading. At first, the roles are clear, with each person trying both roles. Afterward, when we ask which role people preferred, some will report that they liked following more, some leading, and some will enjoy both. If I assume that everyone enjoys leading as much as I do, I will be making a mistake. Some people thrive on following.

Our experience is so particular. Our families, where we grew up, our appearance and our abilities, how other people have treated us, our education, who we love—all these are elements of who we are, what we do and believe, and how we react to one another. If I grew up in a poor family with several brothers and sisters in the Midwest, and you were the only child of well–to–do parents in New York City, we will likely have very different ways of looking at the world.

We can celebrate that rich diversity. It is good that we carry such different stories in our bodyspirits. I can have my story and you can have yours. They don't need to compete.

**It is important to be aware that different experience will lead to different beliefs.** You can almost always trace philosophical, theological, or political disputes about the truth back to differences in personal experience. You and I may believe passionately in opposing points of view, each completely true to us because they are based on our own experience.

**InterPlay teaches us about having fullness—being able to be completely who we are.** It shows us that there is room for every-

> • • • • • • • • •
> If every bodyspirit is different, we may have very different experiences. If we have different experience, we are likely to have different opinions and beliefs.

one to have that. I think we fear that if we take up too much "space," then we will get in the way of others, so we better hold back. Or, if you and I want conflicting things that we must merge into some middle ground to solve the problem.

Through InterPlay we realize that there is plenty of room—more than we realized at first. At the beginning of a class, we have participants walk randomly throughout the entire room. No matter how many people there are, we can still avoid running into each other. Then if we ask everyone to find the edges of the space as well as the center, suddenly the room seems even more spacious, because we haven't really been using all the space there is. Spaciousness is not only physical, but spiritual, intellectual, and emotional as well. We can experience all manner of spaciousness.

**If we have time and space to savor our fullness, it is easy to allow others to savor theirs as well.** Generosity flows from a sense of abundance. If we feel like our resources are limited, we may feel that we have nothing to spare for others. But abundance is subjective. I may have lots and still not experience abundance, or have little and be very generous. We actually have a choice between looking at the world from the point of view of scarcity or abundance. To choose the latter creates more room for fullness.

It may be better for us to take turns having fullness rather than compromising and only getting part of what we need in order to accommodate someone else. When I go to movies with my friend, he likes to sit in a different place than I do. Rather than trying to find seats that are only somewhat satisfying to each of us, we take turns at successive movies choosing exactly where we want to sit. That way I have the satisfaction of sitting right where I want part of the time, and the satisfaction of knowing he is sitting right where he wants the rest of the time.

We have people play with following and leading in pairs. In the beginning the roles are clearly assigned and turns are taken. Later, though, we don't identify who is following and who is leading—we let the roles shift back and forth. The first response for most pairs is to try to move precisely together, with neither person clearly leading. The movement tends to be slow and predictable, and the pairs need to be in constant eye contact with each other. Eventually, they discover (or we point out to them) that it is possible to still have clear initiation and clear following. This usually leads to more interesting interactions. Rather than each person pulling in to accommodate, each can have opportunities to initiate strongly and to follow faithfully.

**InterPlay teaches us to figure out what we want and to create more of it for ourselves, or to ask for help in getting it.** This is a surprisingly easy thing to do. It also helps us have fullness. By paying attention to our body data and knowledge we practice noticing what we enjoy, what is good for us, what gives us energy, what gives us a sense of grace. Then we learn that we have some control over getting more of that. There is much that we can do to get what we want and need.

InterPlay also includes helping others get what they need. Often we need community to get what we want. It is great fun and highly satisfying to help others figure that out. In the process we know that others will help us get what we want and need.

> • • • • • • • • •
> There is no way that we can prepare ourselves in advance for everything that is going to happen to us. To trust that we will know what to do, because we have practiced responding in the moment, is a huge resource.

**InterPlay teaches us to trust our inner resources.** To improvise means that we experiment with creating stuff on the spot. We don't plan and we don't rework things over and over. Depending on the task that is given me, will I know what to do? Will I have something to say? Will I have a story, a song, or a dance? The more we play with this, the more we realize how much information we are carrying around—that there are ideas at the tip of our tongues that we barely know are there. All sorts of stuff comes up in the moment that would be difficult if not impossible to anticipate or plan.

**This teaches us that when the time comes, we will know what to do, regardless of the situation.** Life is always throwing surprises in our path. There is no way that we can prepare ourselves in advance for everything that is going to happen to us. To trust that we will know what to do, because we have practiced responding in the moment, is a huge resource. We don't have to worry nearly as much as we do. We don't need to have everything planned down to the last detail.

**InterPlay converts crises into opportunities for creative response.** It also teaches us that others have resources we can draw on in challenging times.

**InterPlay teaches us to decrease judgment of ourselves and others.** Practicing affirmation turns down the volume of the critical voices that we carry around inside us. It is a gradual process, but an effective one. We release expectations of ourselves and others. To look for the good increases the good in our lives. We realize that others are not here on the earth to do things our way, to fulfill our needs, to satisfy our desires.

To realize that I don't have to critique everything and everybody makes a tremendous difference to me. I am so much more able to enjoy my life.

**InterPlay teaches us about choice.** We learn that within any situation there are tons of options—lots of different ways of doing things. We have more ideas than we know what to do with. And from those many possibilities we can choose. We are not limited to one option. We have many. It teaches us that within any parameters there are infinite possibilities. No matter what our limits are, there are still many things we can do. Even if I can only move one arm, I can move it in a million different ways.

**InterPlay teaches us about control.** What parts of our lives do we have control over? In what areas do we have choice? What do we need to let go of? Life is unpredictable. It is not surprising that we would try to corral it. But our ability to shape events (or other people) is limited. InterPlay presents an alternative. It gives us practice in being able to respond to whatever comes up—to take the information in the moment and make something of it for our own good and that of others. It teaches us flexibility and increases our ability to respond.

**InterPlay teaches us the value of play.** In our culture "work" is an overriding paradigm. We look at so much of our lives from the point of view of work. What if we chose to look through the lens of play instead? What if we chose ease instead of difficulty, joy instead of struggle, possibilities instead of limits, cooperation instead of competition? It is quite possible, you know.

This doesn't mean that life will be without difficulty, challenge, or disappointment. Play includes all of these experiences as well. But it doesn't focus or dwell on them, and that makes a huge difference.

> • • • • • • • • •
> **If money is the center of our motivation and the symbol of our accomplishment, it will overshadow all the other ways that our activities feed us or create grace for ourselves and others.**

**Play includes grace in a way that work often cannot.** To learn to savor experience for what it is, to have inner satisfaction is hard when there is so much focus on product and result. If money is the center of our motivation and the symbol of our accomplishment, it will overshadow all the other ways that our activities feed us or create grace for ourselves and others.

If you pay attention, you will notice that work and play are probably intertwined in your life. They are not really polar opposites or exclusive of each other. What if you focused on the parts of your life that give you satisfaction and joy and tried to increase them, either in large or small ways? For example, what parts of your job do you particularly enjoy? Which people do you enjoy working with? What have you done recently that has been particularly satisfying? Celebrate those things. Name them to yourself. Let others know. Are there ways to have more of any of that?

**Play expands the territory of the present.** It teaches us to be on our toes, to be ready, to pay attention. In our culture, the present has been squashed flat between the past and the future. We live so much in either of those directions that we forget about right now. To learn to respond in the moment is excellent "present" practice. It turns out that **the present is full of delightful surprises, unexpected ideas, and unimagined possibilities.** It is also full of truth and revelation. We discover new things about ourselves, each other, and the world.

**InterPlay teaches us that we can experience life as a whole rather than as separate parts.** We can "have" everything together, that it isn't our job to pull everything apart and analyze it. It teaches us that life is a mystery, and that we can savor that mystery. We don't need to understand everything. We can look at the world in "easy focus," that ability to take in what is around us and enjoy, rather than a "hard focus," which leads us to analysis, judgment, and critique. **In InterPlay the categories of mind, heart, body, and spirit disappear.**

# Conclusion

**We can have fullness in our lives.** We can have more energy, grace, joy, community, fun, peace, connection, and spirit. We can be fed.

Becoming aware of the marvelous particularity of our own experience and at the same time our body–to–body connection with others is a journey toward wholeness. **We can no longer afford to ignore the splits in our lives, in our language, and in our culture.** We must become observant and articulate about what goes on in our own bodies and in the community body.

We must be free to claim the entire interwoven tapestry of our experience. **It is so rich.** It is so subtle and mysterious. When the internal or external voices tempt us to dismiss or deny important parts of ourselves or others, we can resist.

To change may seem daunting if we look at the big cultural picture, but chances are we are already finding the simple practices in our own lives that move us toward integration. We can continue that journey, paying attention to small steps headed in the right direction. **Remember to carry with you the tools of ease and amusement as you go.**

**The desire for change must be our choice.** Making that decision is a crucial part of the process. Remember, though, that changing your mind, like all other spiritual disciplines, is not a single event. It is a continuing practice and must be combined with other physical practices.

You may not be ready to play yet, to throw your whole body into it, but do what you can do. Take the ideas here that are helpful and make an effort to incorporate them into your life.

**You, too, can have it all.**

●●●●●●●●●●●●●●●●●●●●●●●●●●●●●●●●●●●●●●●●●●●●●●●●●●

**Body Wisdom Inc.** is a non–profit corporation co–directed by Cynthia Winton–Henry and Phil Porter devoted to the reintegration of body and spirit through performance, teaching, and writing.

The activities of this organization include workshops and classes using the **InterPlay** technique; **WING IT! Performance Ensemble**, a company which improvisationally blends dance, theater, and music; **WING IT! Press**, which publishes a variety of books, videos and audio tapes; the **InterPlay Leadership Program**, a mentoring program for leadership development and personal growth; and **Wisdom of the Body groups** which provide tools and practices for healing.

Cynthia and Phil travel all over the world **keynoting, teaching, and performing** for many different organizations, colleges and universities, religious institutions, conferences, and health care settings. They also teach **week–long workshops** at various times of the year in the San Francisco Bay Area.

**For booking information**, for a current schedule of activities and classes, or for details about the InterPlay Leadership Program call **Cynthia at 510/814–9584**.

**To order books** or to inquire about other resources offered by Body Wisdom, Inc. contact **Phil Porter at 510/465–2797**.

**Body Wisdom, Inc.**
669A 24th Street
Oakland, CA 94612

phone: 510/465–2797
fax: 510/836–3312
email: pporter316@aol.com